I Was 1

The sound of trees crashing and hoofs pounding were louder than the sound of my heart beating in my ears, and I dropped to one knee so that I could see under the heavy brush.

Coming at me in a fury, was the animal I had been tracking all afternoon. There are times in a person's life, when time itself stands still, and I wondered what Daniel Boone would have done in this situation.

In a fraction of a second my mind went back to the fall of 1959, my dad had just announced that we were going to move to Alaska and get some of that" Free land" the government was giving away under the homestead act, one hundred and sixty acres of some of the best timber land in the world.

Walt Disney had just released two movies, Daniel Boone and Davy Crockett, and I had spent hard earned money to see them over and over again at the local theater. I never got tired of watching the adventures of my two wild back woods Heros, so to a twelve year old boy, the news that we were moving to Alaska was a dream come true.

On the first day of May, 1960, we pulled out of Guymon Oklahoma, leaving the windblown prairie, and headed into the unknown in a 1949 Chevy pickup, loaded with everything we were going to need the first year in this new land. "ALASKA!" Even the word sent shivers of excitement coursing through me.

The sight of us lumbering along the most crooked road in the world, called the Alcan Highway must have been quite a thing to see, I was really glad we didn't own any chickens, or they would have been tied to the truck to. The Beverly hillbillies had nothing on us. The trip alone was an unforgettable experience, and one burned deeply in to my mind.

Early in the evenings our little caravan consisting of three pickup trucks with homemade campers, ours, my grand daddies, and uncle Everettes, would stop at some river or stream to make camp for the night. The men would start working on the trucks, doing the maintenance that was needed to keep them moving up the highway. The women would start supper and all us kids would go fishing or exploring.

After 26 days of this, we pulled into Anchor Point Alaska, over two hundred miles from the nearest paved road. We were tired of being cooped up in that homemade camper and we had finally reached our destination.... Well almost..... We still had six miles of four wheel drive trail called the North Fork road, then six miles of muskeg, mud and a river crossing to our chosen piece of heaven on the bank of the Chacock River.

Dad had marked out our homestead on a map sitting at the kitchen table in Oklahoma, and had no concept of just how remote we would be, and how terribly hard it would be on my mother.

The very next day after arriving, Dad met a homesteader with a small dozer that volunteered to drag our truck through the mud to our homestead. Before the realization of just how isolated we were hit us, we were there, committed to perish or survive. To me it was pure joy, I can still smell the smoke of that first campfire of dead spruce. An aroma I love to smell to this day almost fifty years later, but I think my mom had other ideas of what joy was. I'm think she put a lot of value in running water, elect heat, and a cook stove that did not require wood as an energy source.

I don't think my Mother was impressed by the mosquito infested out house, or spending most of her first winter sleeping, and trying to stay warm under a moose hide cover that she did not have the strength to push off of her.

Dad built a two story house out of green lumber that we had sawed on my uncle's big commercial mill. The only insulation was the boards and tar paper. So when we built a fire in the barrel heater and warmed the house up, all the boards shrunk leaving a large gap where the only thing between us and the outside, was a thin strip of the tarpaper. When it was -30 outside it was about 0 inside.

I remember that it was raining when we moved in the house about the first of November and there was a low spot in the kitchen that held a pool of water. It soon froze and did not thaw until April, even though she cooked all our meals on a wood cook stove not five feet away and the barrel heater was kept roaring constantly. So my poor momma froze all the time we were at the homestead. But to a Daniel Boone wannabe it was pure heaven.

We worked hard in those first years. My brothers and I would cut wood with a cross cut saw and haul it in with our dog team, which consisted of "Tippy" a Collie/Coyote mix that we had brought with us, "Pal" a Lab/Husky mix and a thirty pound Siberian husky female we called Sweetie Pie.

All of the water we used was carried from the spring about a quarter mile away in buckets. All food supplies were carried the six miles from the gravel road on military packs on our backs.

With a 3006 hung on a sling on my shoulder, a 22 Winchester cradled in my arms and knives of all kinds strapped all over me, I roamed those hills and creeks for miles around our homestead until I knew every inch of it by heart.

I watched the life and death struggle of bears taking down moose calves from our front porch that over looked the river bottom. I saw the otters play for hours on end sliding down their snow and mudslides into the creek just below the house. I saw coveys of spruce hens that numbered into the hundreds, and watched King Salmon spawn in the frigid waters of the Chacock River.

I practiced and honed my hunting, fishing and tracking skills until I am quite sure old Dan Boone would have been proud of me. I provided about ninety nine percent of all the meat and fish our family of four consumed until I got married and moved out.

The sound of the charging animal brought me back to the reality at hand, and not fifty feet and closing fast was the biggest bull moose I had ever seen, eyes glazed with a red hue, that told of his frustration at being so persistently pursued, and in a final desperate act had turned and charged.

I had seen the moose cross the road in front of us on our way back from town. As soon as we got to the house I grabbed my gun and took off running back to the point where he had crossed the road. In those days I never went anyplace without both coat pockets full of biscuits, because I never knew where I was going to be next. Once on his track I was relentless, I had learned that a bull will always stop on the other side of the first clearing he comes to, and look back to see what's after him, that's when I would usually get a shot, but in my haste to catch up to the moose I came onto the clearing to quickly and he spotted me and took off on the run. I never even got the gun to my shoulder until he was out of sight.

Normally I would have given up at that point because the moose will make about a ten mile loop and wind up back within a hundred yards of where I first saw him, but on this day his fate was sealed. We had been out of meat for a long time, and I was tired of beans and fish. I also knew it was up to me to change the diet, so I settled down and took off after the moose with a determined resolution to get him.

Untold hours of observation and tracking had taught me that, if a moose enters a swamp he would not alter his direction until he reached the other side and entered the woods. I had also learned that a bull will urinate on the run, while a cow on the other hand will squat and pee in one spot.

When tracking a moose in the winter this was a good thing to know. I also learned to observe the depth of the tracks and a thousand other things that are buried in my subconscious.

Again I was jerked back to reality and suddenly I knew what Daniel Boone would have done, so I took a deep breath and calmly sighted my old 30-06 spring field, and squeezed the trigger. The bullet hit him right between the eyes and he fell five feet in front of me. That is one time that a miss would have meant sure death for me, it was just too close for comfort, even for Daniel Boone I think.

It took thirty minutes for the adrenalin to subside to the point where I could quit shaking.

I had been so deeply engrossed in the tracking and stalking of the big moose, that I had no idea where I was in relation to the road. I was really starting to dread the long pack out. Finally when I reached down to cut his throat and start the cleaning process, I noticed through the trees I could see a flash of white, and after closer investigation I discovered it was our house. The moose had made the big circle and came back to within two hundred yards of our house. I have had some luck in my many years of hunting and fishing in Alaska but this was "One for the books" as my old grand daddy put it.

Old Ron

I don't know why, but it seems like I was always

getting into situations that don't happen to regular normal people, and it was a constant that I could depend on throughout my life. Any one that knows me knew that they could count on me to be ready to hook up my dogs and go on some hair brained adventure on a moment's notice.

I have known old Ron for as long as I have been in this North Country, and over a period of years I learned some valuable life lessons from that retired, World War 2 pilot.

Probably the most important thing I got from him; was that one can push the human body so far past the normal limits we set for ourselves, that we don't even fit in the range of normal anymore. What most people call extreme pain, he viewed as an inconvenience. Pain is relevant Ron would say, it lets us know we are still alive.

Now Webster's defines relevant as-- "Relating to the matter under consideration; pertinent" So I guess using his logic, pain was related to life and a necessary element, if you can call pain an element.

Ron had some quirky little ways that I did not even try to understand, one being that when a favorite lead dog died from old age, he would skin it and nail the hide to the side of his shed. Most of the people who visited him at his homestead, thought it barbaric. I did to and after I had known him for many years, I finally felt comfortable enough in our friendship to ask him one day why he did it. His reply shocked me speechless.

He was so fond of that particular dog, that when it's hide hung on his shed, he could look out his window and see it every day. It served as a marker of time in his life as well as a memory trigger.

"When I look at their hides on that shed Mel, I can remember not only the dog, but the beautiful places I've been and the things I've seen and done. There's one nailed up there that has a red coat that I called Tosh, and he caused me more grief than any lead dog I ever had. Once on the

Iditarod he chewed every harness off every dog, and I had to go around to the locals buying harness, and half of them didn't fit properly. Or the time he bred a female at the start of the Iditarod at Mulchady Park, and I had to sit there while they were connected for thirty minutes with two hundred people laughing at me from the bleachers, man that was embarrassing, but those times are good memories now. I have to admit they sure weren't when they were happening though." and he threw back his head and laughed so hard he had tears in his eyes just remembering the dog and his temperament. I knew that was a true story because I was there and laughed along with the other two or three hundred people even though I was in the same race. I had drawn out ten places behind him and got to see the whole show…..Dotty his wife, in the basket trying to look so casual with her face as red as it can get, and Ron cussing the dogs trying to hurry up the process.

How in the world can you argue with his kind of logic? That wall on his shed was a history of his life in Alaska, and all it took to rekindle a memory was a glance out his window. All of a sudden I realized I was getting a rare view into the complex nature of the man I thought I had known really well for such a long time.

Driving a dog team today is nothing like it was in those days. Today even running the Iditarod which is the longest dogsled race in the world, they go 10 miles an hour for three or four hours on a trail marked so well a blind man could follow it, then stop at a checkpoint and eat warm food provided by the locals.

But in those early days of the Iditarod, the trail markers were merely survey ribbon tied to a tree or willow branch and by the next day the wind had blown them away, and the musher's packed their own food with them on the sled. I only mention this to point out that back then a long distance musher was a survivor by necessity, and tough as nails, and Ron ran the very first race when no one knew where they were going and blazed the trail as they went.

In the old days each trip we took away from home was an adventure in itself. Our dogsleds were packed with enough dog food to last the entire trip, start to finish. Axe, snowshoes, extra clothes in case we fell into overflow, and usually a gun of some kind, and after that first trip with Ron I usually had enough food for myself and Ron. He would sure eat it if I had it, but as long as I knew him, he would never, ever, pack any for himself other than an orange. Those trips were slow, and we spent as much time on snowshoes in front of the team, as we did on the runners. We got to really see the country and wildlife.

One day not long after I had met Ron, I got a lesson I never forgot. He showed up at my house one morning with a dog team, and sled packed full of supplies for a trapper who lived at Skwentna, which is a remote settlement about 40 miles up the Yentna River.

"Hook up seven dogs and bring your sleeping bag, and lets hit the trail this is going to be an overnighter," Ron said grinning from ear to ear.

It was in fact a 70 mile cross country trip from my house with no existing trail, and the snow was three feet deep. "How much food do I need to bring?" I asked, "I got plenty of snack things I can pack in my duffle bag."

Ron grinned and said, "Don't bother, I have all we need. Hurry we got to go get across the Big Su before dark!" So I didn't pack any food, or water, or anyone of a dozen things I later learned to always have with me on such outings with him. About eight hours into the trip I got really hungry, and when we stopped to rest the dogs, I said, "Ok Ron, drag out the chow." So he reached into his sled and came out with a frozen orange which he tossed to me, and told me to eat my half and give it back. When the orange was gone I told him to get some more food out because I was starving, and he said "That's it nada, no more."

I wanted to kill and eat him I was so mad and

hungry. I must have asked him "How far is it to Skwentna" a thousand times that day and into the night, his answer was always the same, and stayed the same, then, and for all the years to follow, "Bout a mile"

It got so that I looked forward to the times when a new guy would want to come with us, I would send him to Ron for all his questions about what to bring on the trip. I would put the new guy between Ron and myself, so that my mentor would do his usual thing, and ignore whoever was behind him. I would watch the rookie in all his misery, and silently snicker to myself. I was always careful to hold my team back and not to get to close, lest I might have to share my orange.

It was from Ron that I first heard the saying "If you aint the lead dog the scenery never changes."

I remember once when a dog food company we had never heard of, wanted to sponsor Ron and gave him a ton of their dog food for him to test. Now I have no idea what the secret ingredient in their formula was but it made the dogs gaseous and stink to high heaven. They would go down the trail constantly farting. Poor Ron couldn't get me to follow close enough to hear him talk, and when we would stop for a rest he was visibly sick to his stomach smelling those dog farts. For about a month he had the worst smelling dog team in the history of dog mushing, and had to finally give up on the free dog food.

He is also the one who got me back into dog driving again as simply a means of reliable transportation for the remote places we wanted to go.

Growing up on a 160 acre homestead on the Kenai Peninsula in the 1960s, our family depended on the dog team to haul freight in from the highway. We used the dog team on a daily basis for wood, water and transportation, so it was easy for Ron to rekindle my passion of the dog team, and eventually the sport of racing which culminated in me running the 1979 Iditarod Dog Sled Race.

I was really gullible and it took me years to figure out that if I got my dogs from Ron, I would never be able to keep up with him on our trips or beat him in a race. Of course he would only get rid of his slowest dogs or mean fighting ones.

I remember a period of time when I had a really slow team that fought constantly and I had to keep a club in my hand for my own protection. When I would meet other teams on the trail in a head on, they would go away with a memory to tell their grandkids about.

The spring of 1977 Ron showed up early one morning and told me to hook up seven dogs, pack for an overnighter, and bring a rifle. So with that warning I loaded my sled pretty heavy and we took off for the headwaters of sheep creek to check out a gold story some old trapper after one too many beers had told to Ron. But truthfully I think I knew there was no trapper that had told him anything. He had just gotten bored and wanted to go someplace we had never been, and of course he had to twist my arm to get me to go.

When we left familiar country and headed up the sheep creek river basin. The snow was about fifteen feet deep, and made the going pretty easy and fast from daylight until about two pm in spite of the heavy sleds. The days were warm and sunny and the snow melted in the late afternoon, then refroze the next night when the temperature dropped to nearly zero. This caused a hard crust to form on the surface that would support a man's weight from daylight until the sun softened it up by early afternoon.

After we had traveled about fifteen miles upriver we found holes in the creek ice where the warmer natural springs had thawed a circle about fifty feet in diameter, and the moose would go off down in there to get a drink of water, then they could not get out because of the steep sides, and if a bear did not get them first, then they would starve to death.

On that trip we watched a big grizzly kill, and drag back to his den, a large moose that could not get out of the creek on his own. We saw the awesome power of the Grizzly bear that day and found some new respect for the animal.

Now Ron had a lead dog named "Barron" and a better lead dog had never been born, but he had only one real problem, He hated moose---he hated them with a passion, and once he spotted a moose he had only one thing in his mind and that was to attack. Nothing else existed in his small brain but that moose. He could instill that passion into all the rest of the dogs equally by the third bark with the diligence of a drill sergeant.   Now Barron feared only one thing that I knew of, and that was of a gun being fired. I think he may have had good reason to fear that sound knowing Ron as I did. We were making good time and seeing lots of nice country, when all of a sudden Ron's team took off on a hard run barking like demons. My team woke up and started following. I saw old Barron barking and frothing at the mouth, and when I looked on past him I saw another one of those holes in the river, and it had a full grown moose trapped. I could barely hold on to my sled I was laughing so hard.

Ron had a death grip on the handle bow, his foot hard on the brake, and the resulting rooster tail went thirty feet into the air. It was a sight to behold, and I got to thinking…. what if old Barron jumped right out into the air onto the moose's back, which was just below our level of trail. I didn't know what to do, so at the very last second I pulled my 44 magnum pistol out, and leaned way out to the left so as not to hit Ron. Then just as Barron bunched all his muscles to jump, I fired, and the bullet kicked up the snow between him and the moose, which was by now about fifteen feet away.

Barron never lost stride, he just turned an abrupt right, and went straight up the mountain. When he had gotten as far straight up as he could go, he would go around and around a clump of willows until he had the team so tangled it would take an hour for Ron to get them back down on the river, and past the moose.

The whole time Ron would be screaming curse words and all sorts of profanities that haven't even been invented yet, and all of them directed at old Barron. "Why did you do that Mel? I coulda stopped him," Ron yelled.
I tried to reason with him until I just gave up, "If this happens again I won't shoot until you tell me to, and then I might not just for meanness after all this ungratefulness". We didn't go two miles before Barron picked up the scent of another moose and took off again, only this time the moose was under a tree, with only his back visible because of the depth of the snow. Ron new the moose was healthy and ready to defend his ground so he started hollering "Shoot Mel, shoot---dammit---shoooooooot!"

I got such a kick out of waiting until the last second, out of sheer meanness, and the fact that I was laughing so hard at Ron and His thirty foot ice brake rooster tail, that I almost waited too long. But when I finally shot, the result was the same with the old lead dog. He made a right turn and headed up the mountain on a dead run, and again around and around some willows. That happened four times before we got to the wall of rock just below the glacier and as far you can go without some mountain climbing gear.

I had laughed so hard on that trip that my sides were sore for weeks after, and Ron had to do a lot of praying to get back on the Lords good side because of his language.
I only had one incident on that trip, and the night before we left on the return trip home I had a female come into heat. When we got camp made, and the dogs fed and bedded down for the night Ron told me he was going to be laughing at me in the morning. I didn't understand what he meant until I woke up at daybreak.

I had tied up the male with a dog chain and left all the females on the gang line made of poly. Well the male grabbed the gang line after we were sleeping, and pulled the whole team of 6 females and sled towards him. Then he would stop and chew all the lines into. Then pull some more, stop and chew some more, until he got to the female that was in heat.

All that sex must have made him hungry, because then he tugged on the sled until it was close enough, then he got into my sled bag and ate all my food. How he towed that sled with the ice hook stuck in the snow I'll never know, but it had plowed a furrow in the packed snow for twenty feet.

The next morning he was so tired he didn't want to work in the team so I showed him I still had the 44 mag. and he went right to work. Of course this was after I listened to Ron laugh until he spit up blood. Then I tied all those pieces of gang line back together and let the female in heat just run free. Because the male must have liked his women naked, he had chewed her harness completely off her, all that was left was a pile of short pieces and a ring of harness material around her neck.

I was so mad at the dog that I tied and extra knot in his tug line so that every time the dog in front of him jumped over anything in his way, "Humper" as I called him after that, got stretched out like an accordion. Not dangerously so but extremely uncomfortable. After my mad subsided, I stopped and untied the extra knots, and things went back to normal.

On that trip after talking to all the old timers we knew, I can safely say that Ron and I went where no one had ever taken a dog team. At least that's what we like to think.

We saw lots of moose, two big Grizzlies just waking up from the winter's hibernation and ravenously hungry, more ptarmigan and spruce grouse than I could ever count, and we saw Alaska, virgin in her splendid glory, and raw rugged beauty.

We didn't find any gold; Ron didn't even unpack his gold pan. I did make a half hearted attempt, that lasted for about five minutes in that ice cold stream before I froze out and stopped panning due to a sudden loss of interest. As I said before we just went because we had never been there.

Ron owned an airplane not particularly designed for bush pilots, because it had a short wing span and needed lots of runway. It had a fairly fast stall speed, and most of the landings we made on river bars or abandoned air strips turned into a few seconds of terror for both of us.

Ron would show up at my house and say hey lets go see where the caribou are on the Denali, it almost hunting season. That's all the excuse I needed, so we were off, flying the Denali highway, spotting caribou and moose for the hunt I would go on in a few weeks. One thing though, I always made him take the time to put the other control stick in the plane. A matter that only took a few minutes, that way if he fell over dead from a heart attack or stroke, I at least had a fighting chance of landing somewhere. Eventually I learned enough that I am quite sure I could have landed safely.

Over the years I flew with him in all kinds of weather and every time we went up I always got to fly the plane for a while. He said I was a natural because I was an equipment operator, used to working joy sticks on backhoes. I don't know how much truth is in all that; only that over the years I learned to fly an airplane, and get the hell scared out of me occasionally.

One day Ron came over and asked me if I would go with him to help pack out a moose. At the time Ron was pretty heavy into religion and had taken a missionary Baptist preacher from Oklahoma moose hunting. The guy knocked down a huge bull. I assumed then and I still think that he charged the preacher a healthy sum of money. The preacher told me that he had been promised someone to pack out the moose. Anyway I agreed to go help.

Ron had borrowed a super cub from one of our friends, and we took off at Montana Lake. When we got to altitude Ron headed for a lake in the upper Susitna Valley on the western side.

Sure enough the preacher shot a record size bull moose about a mile from the lake. Packing that big moose down to the lake tested my strength and endurance and after I got it all down to the lake, Ron started making trips back to Montana Lake with heavy loads of meat, and I mean heavy loads.

Just before take off with the last load of meat and preacher, Ron hit a rock and snagged a hole in the right float, the weather was getting windy and it was raining heavily.

I said, "Do not leave me here alone all night, I don't even have a sleeping bag." we had already sent the camp out, but I knew he was thinking about telling me he would be back in the morning to pick me up, and when he said so I was ready for him, I screamed "You aint leaving me here all night in the f****** rain with no gear or rifle in bear country with fresh moose blood all around me.''

He finally agreed to come back for me, and I relaxed because I knew, that he knew, that I would shoot him if he didn't come back for me. Normally I would have stayed there overnight but because of where we were (In the land of huge Grizzlies with a blood trail right to me) and the fact I had no shelter or food, or rifle. I had made my mind up I was not going to stay, and that was that! So I watched as he took off, noticing how labored and sluggish the plane was, getting air born. When he circled back and few over me I saw the water pouring out of the hole in the float…it was bad.

When he finally faded in the distance I settled in for the long wait, huddled down under a tree, the only shelter I could find from the constant rain.

Darkness was approaching fast and I had almost given up when I heard the sound of the little Super-cub approaching. Instantly went from cussing him to thinking what a fine fellow he was to come back in this storm to get me. By the time he was on the lake it was a full blown storm.

As he taxied in, the wind blew him into the same

rock he had hit earlier and split the already dangerously flooded float, tearing a much bigger hole. (How he managed to hit the exact same spot on the float is another mystery that will remain unsolved.) That's when our adventure really started. Ron ran the plane up as far as he could onto a short stretch of beach and we started hand pumping the water out of it. It took an hour and I thought we were ok, but when we pushed the plane of the beach and got in and found the seat belts and got them secured, the float promptly sunk. We had to get the plane back on the beach and repeated the same pumping job.

When we were ready to take off I told Ron to get in and start the motor, and as soon as I pushed the plane off the beach, to start the take off instantly at full throttle, and not to worry about me as I would climb in while he was getting the leaking float off the water. I said it shouldn't take more than 30 seconds with the choppy water on the lake to get airborn. I almost never got him to agree to such a plan, this man was a retired ww2 war pilot and had thousands of military "by the book" flying hours.

When we were ready I pushed the plane off of the beach and Ron pushed the throttle wide open, and I scrambled to get on the float. When we took off up the lake, he would lift the airplane off the water about five feet and I would grab the door and start to get in. Suddenly we would hit the water so hard I would almost fall overboard.

All this time we were gaining airspeed, and I was being whipped by the water spray from the prop wash, then slammed down to the float almost losing my balance. This happened about ten times, we would get about five or six feet off the water then bam we would hit the water again, about the time I would get my balance I would lose it. Finally I got hold of the door handle and I wasn't turning loose.

I drug myself up to where I could see what was going on. Ron would pull the stick back and we would lift off, then he would turn loose of the stick and start trying to hook his seat belt. About the time he would get it all lined up to snap the ends together the plane would take a nose dive, and hit the water so hard he would be forced to turn loose of the seat belt and pull the stick back again. Never mind me outside getting drowned, and the hell beat out of me while hanging on for dear life, and leaving claw marks in the fuselage…. no…. he had to get that damn seat belt fastened.

Well you could have heard me scream at him clear down in Montana. "Forget that M***** F******* seat belt, you can hook it later after I am in the F******plane and we have some f****** altitude."

After all we were running out of lake, and we still were not staying airborne. After he realized what he was doing, he finally kept the plane in the air, and I was able to get in.

All of the strict military training, and by the manual flying he had done for so many years, had almost gotten us killed that day. Later when we were at H&H lodge sipping hot coffee, I asked him why he was so intent on fastening that seat belt, and he said, "I sure don't know. It's like my brain went south, I was in a trance I guess, and if you hadn't yelled and cursed at me like you did, we probably would have crashed at the end of the lake."

It was not the shrill high pitched scream which sounded like it was coming from a teenage girl that got his attention that night….. No…. it was the foul cursing that finally got through to his scrambled brain..Why? Because Ron was a religious man, an ordained minister, and the foul language that I used in that high pitched girlie voice is what finally brought him out of his self induced coma.

With that one exception, I do have to say that Ron was probably was the safest, most knowledgeable pilot I have ever flown with.

In the1979 Iditarod dogsled race there were a lot of dog

teams in the race and each had his own reason for being there. For Ron and I it was just a trail that someone had put in for us to go on a twelve hundred mile camping trip with the dogs. We did not race to win, we raced each other, and right off the bat Ron got the jump on me when I followed my brother Steve who was also running the race, down a wrong trail twenty miles from the start.

Going into the first checkpoint at Su Station, I signed the check sheet as the last man in the race. When I would get to a check point I didn't look to see who was in the lead or how far they were in front of me---I looked for Ron's time and place. I went on a four hour on, and four hour off running schedule which is good for the dogs but a man killer.

Out of the four hours off, the musher has to get the water hot and cook dog food and then feed them before he can lay in the sled basket for a short rest, then he has to get up and feed and water the dogs again, then pack all the gear away and put booties on all of the dogs before heading down the trail.

I would make a little progress gaining on Ron, twenty minutes here and an hour there until I eventually caught up with him on the Yukon River just out of Blackburn on the way to Kaltag.

I rounded a bend in the river and there he was lying in his sleeping bag snoring.

I didn't know it then, but he had been watching the sign in sheet at the checkpoints also, and his only concern was where I was. He didn't want his protégé to catch him and beat him to Nome, and he was doing his very best to keep that from happening.

When I got him awake and on his feet, I saw that he was coughing constantly and spitting up blood, and I worried the rest of the race he might die on the trail. He had pneumonia and had had it for a week. A normal man would have scratched, quitting the race, but not Ron, he was nowhere near a normal man. He finished the race never stopping to rest. I did beat him to Nome, but only because I was running a borrowed dog team, a very very good borrowed dog team, and they took me to the finish line in sixteenth place, which was a respectable position considering I was a rookie using someone else's dogs I had gotten a month before the race started.

A few days after the race was over, I was bellied up to the counter at Nome Joes, busy replacing the thirty pounds I had lost on the race with hamburgers and milkshakes. Ron, who I thought was near death with pneumonia, was headed towards Point Barrow leading a few other dog teams, to bring publicity to the plight of the Eskimos and their right to hunt whales.

I would like to think that that was the only reason he did it, but I know Ron too well. No one had ever driven a dog team from Anchorage to Point Barrow via Nome. I would have went with him, I sure wanted to, but the wife I had then was at the finish line in Nome waiting for me, and she had "had enough" of dogs for one year, that is the only time that he ever asked me to go some place with him that I had to refuse. There was an old drunk Eskimo in the bar that day that offered to trade me his best lead dog for my wife…damn…too bad hind sight is twenty twenty. I could have used a good leader.

The day after thanksgiving every year, Ron would load his wife Dorothy on his sled and I would follow with my team, we would have a bottle of Brandy or Peppermint Schnapps each and go visiting the people living in the bush that we knew. These trips would last all night long, going from one house to another visiting and drinking. In my mind I can still see the crystal clear sky with the stars so bright and the moon looking like you could reach out and touch it as we slid through the woods and swamps with the only sound being the swoosh of the runners on fresh snow and the panting of dogs.

We would stop briefly at each house, visiting and

sampling their homebrew, and when we would get back to Ron's house in the wee hours of the next morning, we would all be snot slinging commode hugging drunk. I spent many nights sleeping on their floor to drunk to go home after those trips to visit people that lived far from civilization. I was really glad when he got his religion back and quit drinking, but those were sure some good times.

Old Ron was the toughest man I have ever known, and I am proud to have been his friend. Together he and I got to see a part of Alaska that very few will ever see or experience. In 1986 Ron got to live his greatest dream of running the Yukon Quest dogsled race, when many thought his racing days were long past.

But I know the real reason he entered that race, and it was because…. simply put---a thousand mile dogsled trail in a part of Alaska he had never seen, and that beckoned to him---and its call was irresistible.

March 27th 1964 earthquake

March 27th, 1964, at 5:36 pm I was at home with my folks in a log cabin on the North Fork road that we were staying in during breakup, when I heard a loud rumbling that sounded like a train coming through the house. I looked out our window to the north up a long swamp, and saw the ground coming in ten foot high waves like I have seen in the ocean. I started trying to get out of the house as the first waves hit us.

I almost got to the door when I was thrown off my feet. I kept trying to get up and out the door, but kept getting thrown back to the floor. Six minutes is a long time to wait for the earth to quit shaking, and honestly I thought the world was being torn apart and we all would die. The shaking just would not end

When the earthquake finally got over with, the old log cabin was still intact most likely because it was a log house. Years later we found out that our earthquake had been upgraded to a 9.1 and shook for 6 full minutes...The strongest and longest lasting earthquake ever recorded on the North American Continent.

My little brother Steve was in the outhouse when it hit and thought a bear had came out of hibernation and was shaking the outhouse trying to get to him.

The next day I headed out from Anchor Point in my old 1954 Ford to see what changes the earthquake the day before had made. The Anchor River Bridge on the North Fork had been knocked out and I had to start up our old D-4 Cat dozer, and drive it to the river and tow my car across to the other side. The road had cracks and holes but I drove around them and made it to Homer with no trouble.

Radio reports were still pretty haphazard, and these were the days before television had made it to Homer, but we did hear that the Homer Spit had sunk six feet. There was not as much in the news about damage to the lower Kenai Peninsula, as there was about the widespread destruction in Anchorage, Seward, Kodiak and Valdeze. They had taken such a beating that the news was mostly about them. In actuality we were the same distance from the epicenter as Anchorage was with the same geological makeup of earth under us.

In Anchorage there were people who were looking for missing family members. There were houses that had slid off their foundations or into huge cracks in the earth. There were boats that had disappeared with crew members still on board.

Locomotive engines in Seward had been tossed half way up a mountain like they were toys by the huge tidal wave that was produced by the mountains on both sides of the bay. Loss of life in those hard hit areas were being tallied on an hourly basis.

It seemed that if we had a tidal wave in Kachemak bay we would have heard by now. Living at Anchor Point on much higher ground, and 27 miles away from the bay we would not have seen any evidence of a wave but we had definitely felt the shake. I pushed on.

As I made my way onto the Homer Spit, I noticed cracks in the pavement but nothing major. The bay lay glassy calm before me with gas barrels floating around on the surface. Probably came from the Standard Oil yard on the end of the spit I reasoned. So far so good I said to myself. I drove carefully through the sand and debris that the night tide had deposited on the road.

I suddenly realized that the tide seemed to still be coming in! I tried to hurry but now the water was beginning to cover the road. The land on both sides of the road was already under water. I had never before seen these areas covered with water. Up ahead I could see a dry spot, and was determined to see if I could get there before the water got so deep the car would stall.

I had to slow down because now I had no idea where the road was and the water was still rising at an amazing speed. The patch of land I had been trying to get too disappeared. Panic began to set in. I could see the cannery a few miles away that looked to me like a little house boat with water all around it. I looked behind me, all I could see was water, and I knew I was alone and in big trouble.

Then to add insult to injury the car hesitated and chugged to a final stop. There was water in the floorboard of the car now and my feet were getting wet. I was stranded…If I could swim, which I could not do in that cold water, I would not know where to swim too. I was two thirds of the way out on the spit and the tide was still coming in fast.

As a last stand I climbed on top of my car. I stood up and noticed a boat headed toward Bluff Point. I tried to hail them. In the process of jumping up and down and waving my arms I mashed the top of my car in. The boat sailed on.

Just when I thought I could not be any more nervous about my situation, the car began to sway a bit in the current of the incoming tide. What if the wind starts blowing!! The very thought made my knees shake. I began saying little prayers. "God are you watching? You know I can't swim to land. If you are not too busy would you see if you could help, I am only 16 and I hope I have a lot of living to do yet."

The car shifted again and I was aware that I was standing in water up to my knees on top of the car. I was so scared I felt brittle... like if I coughed I might just shatter. I wondered if the water was deep enough for a whale, maybe a killer whale might come along and snatch me right off the car. I hoped there were no rogue waves running around out there looking for a place to come ashore. I thought of a thousand things that might happen to a guy in my situation. In every direction I looked all I saw was water except for the cannery which was high and dry some two miles distant. Just when I felt the end was at hand, I heard an outboard motor. In a matter of minutes a small boat came into view, and I realized that someone from the cannery was coming to rescue me. The fellow told me later that he had been using his binoculars watching the tide come in over the road when he spotted me sticking out of the water looking like a tree with two limbs. Man I am glad he had his binoculars that day because in all reality he saved my life.

Dawson Canada and Yellow Gold

In the spring of 1988 I met my current wife Elizabeth, who then was working at H&H lodge as a waitress, I was fresh out of a twenty two year marriage, and going through all the stages of mental recovery that one goes through. She was easy to talk to and fun to be around, and was in all sense of the word, a lost soul, just like me.

We had an extremely cold January that year, with a record temperature of 67 below 0 for 26 days in a row. It was the highest barometric pressure ever recorded on the North American continent and grounded planes in both Anchorage and Fairbanks. You could spit and it would make a cracking sound like that of a .22 rifle, and when it hit the ground it would bounce.

I was living in a cabin way back in the woods which measured 12 by 14 ft, and belonged to my old buddy Ron Aldrich. It was tiny but warm and cozy. I was getting myself back together mentally, and after a year I was starting to feel pretty good about myself.

I spent my days feeding the mice that had invaded the little cabin to escape the extreme cold, cutting firewood for the wood heater, and making sure my moose stew was maintained. Whatever ingredients it needed were added daily. I kept it going 24-7 on the wood heater, and it was responsible in a large part to my success with Lizzie. The stew was made from a recipe I had learned from Ron's wife Dottie, and the secret ingredient was a can of mountain dew. The moose stew was by all standards--- delicious. Liz fell in love with my moose stew first, then me.

When I would get tired of reading Louis L'Amour, I

would fire up my Coleman stove which I kept in the house, then I would take it out and put it under the oil pan of my Datsun pick up for thirty minutes. The truck would start, but then I would have to wait for another thirty minutes with the transmission in neutral, before the grease would soften up enough for me to move the shifter and put it in gear. When I thought I had the truck as warm as I could get it I would then head for H&H to see Lizzie. The little Datsun did not have power steering and at that extreme temperature the grease in the steering box was like concrete and it took all my strength to turn the steering wheel. I would go down the road weaving from side to side, over steering, barely missing the ditch, and my tracks looked like a drunk had driven the truck. Sheer determination got me to the lodge five miles away.

I was sitting in H&H having my daily gallon of coffee, and talking to Lizzie when a guy came in and said he had heard that I might be available to drive his truck for him on the "Yukon Quest" A thousand mile dog race between Fairbanks Alaska, and Whitehorse Canada that alternates direction each year.

A musher entering the race had to have his dog truck at the finish line so that he would have transportation for his team to go home. Some musher's wanted their truck at every checkpoint that had road access for support.

This particular year it was going to end in Whitehorse, and of course I said yes I would love to drive his truck for him along the race route. That is how I came to see Dawson Canada, home of the early Klondike gold rush for the first time

.

When I arrived in Dawson it was February, lots of snow and about -40. Ed, the fellow that had signed up to give me a place to stay while I was there waiting for my musher to come in, took me to the bars and introduced me to the locals, an experience I will treasure always.

The only way I can explain Dawson Canada is this way….. Every place else I have ever been, including most parts of Alaska, gold is a dream, an elusive dream that haunts miners and fortune hunters with an unequaled passion. In Dawson City Canada, gold is a reality… an everyday reality. All of the locals work on gold claims, and mining is the number one topic of conversation in any business establishment you enter.

The only problem I had with the Klondike, is that the ground is permafrost, and only thaws a little in late summer before it refreezes again the next winter. This makes digging extremely hard if not impossible without modern heavy equipment, unless of course you have the strength of mind, body, and character that the old time prospectors had back at the turn of the century, when everything they did was done by hand, and life was hard. Very few of us modern day men possess these admirable traits.

Ed my guide introduced me to a fellow at the Bonanza Bar and Roadhouse that he called "Crazy Pierre." Pierre had not had a bath all winter and was the color of wood smoke, I couldn't tell where his clothes stopped and his skin began. His hair was a tangled mess that reached below his shoulders, and caused him to look like a wild man. He was busy chain smoking cigarettes, and trying to get drunk as fast as he possibly could, and all the while talking 90 miles an hour.

He told us he had a claim out on the Klondike River, and he was "Sinking a shaft." The way this is done is to stack fire wood on the frozen ground, burn it and then shovel out the thawed muck. Then repeat the procedure over and over until the hole either became too deep to work or you hit pay dirt. Well Pierre told us that he was not far from the gold and that he could feel it in his bones. Of course we all laughed and bought him beer and more cigarettes, and he continued to entertain us far into the night.

My experience that winter made me anxious to

return, and explore this interesting place that has such a colorful history.

The next spring I talked it over with Liz and in a few hours we were on our way to Dawson, we took the short cut from just outside of Toke Junction called the top of the world Highway. This road follows a ridge, and you can see for miles and miles on both sides of the road, with the terrain sloping off in a downward flow of elevation, making you feel like you are indeed on the top of the world.

During the course of the winter I had mentioned to Lizzie's step Dad that we might go there in the spring and he told me of a gold mine he had worked on the year before just across the border into Canada. He said he had left some sample bags one day and that they should still be there where he had put them.

He had taken the company dozer down the creek a distance, and then had made a right hand turn and went up on a shelf. Then after ripping the permafrost he had dozed a hole about five feet deep, and took two samples, one from the top of the hole and the other from the bottom. It had impressed him enough to go into Dawson and stake a claim on the ground. So we had that to fall back on if we lost interest in the Klondike.

When we got to the Yukon River we had to ride the ferry across to Dawson. The first person we saw there was wearing a cowboy hat covered with big gaudy gold nuggets, and I could feel the excitement building in me.

I hunted up my friend Ed and in the course of our conversation I asked him what ever happened to crazy Pierre, and he said that crazy Pierre had hit a bonanza of gold. First he dug out all that he could by himself and then sold the claim for one million cash to a big Montana mining outfit. Now "Crazy Pierre" was on the French Riviera, basking in the sunshine, and lighting his cigars with hundred dollar bills.

When we went to the Klondike Bar and Lodge to eat,

the owner found out that Liz was a waitress from our conversation, and promptly offered her a job for really high wages, so she took it and that left me free to explore.

At the start of World War 2 the gold dredges were shut down by the government both in Canada and the USA. And by shutting down I mean shut down right now with no warning. If the bucket was in the ground it stayed there. They just turned off the key and walked away. So I got the idea to go find the dredges, and clean any areas around the riffles and substructures to see what I might find. I am sure I was not the first one to do that, but I still got about 2 ounces per dredge, and I did nothing to threaten the integrity of any of the dredges I explored.

It was an adventure, and its memory is one that I value greatly. Being alone on those mighty gold processing machines with the ghosts of the past was an eerie feeling. They were mammoth in size and hand made on the spot. All of the timbers and steel had to be brought in on Yukon River steamships to Dawson and somehow gotten to the creeks to be dredged.

There were times when I would be working deep in the bowels of one of those dredges, and a soft breeze would be blowing through the substructure of the dredges, I swear I could hear the miners working and the bucket churning.

It is interesting to note that approximately 95 % of all the gold sold from the Klondike during the gold rush era was considered fine gold. The dredges were set up for fine gold recovery using mercury amalgamation as the final method. The larger nuggets went right back out the sluice box, and the largest nugget ever found, was by an elderly tourist lady many years later in the tailing pile on the Klondike river. She was within sight of the Klondike Bar. It was a gold and quartz rock about the size of a basketball. There are still millions and millions of dollars worth of gold waiting …. waiting to be found.

While we were in Dawson City a fellow won the bid

to furnish gravel for the front street road, and he decided to have the gravel assayed because hand panning showed a little color. No one figured it would amount to anything because it was less than a mile from town and half way up a hillside that he had stripped for the gravel pit. Well the assay came back at one hundred dollars a yard.

He had a money making contract with the city of Dawson and a gold claim worth millions. Liz and I would stop and watch his operation. He would load the gravel on trucks and bring it down to the bottom of the hill, then run it through a sluice box to recover the gold. Then he would load the tailings back on the trucks and go dump it on the road project. It is hard for me to understand how that gold went undiscovered so close to town for nearly a hundred years.

All the bars and roadhouses in Dawson kept a set of working gold scales sitting on the bar, and all or most all of the miners that came into town to re-supply or party would pay in gold.

After I had worked all the dredges that I could find, I decided to check out the creek that Lizzie's step dad had told me about. I headed out to the creek, and luckily the road had not washed out from the flood the fall before. When I got there the sample bags were exactly where he said they would be, on the fuel tank boardwalk, a very dangerous place to put a gold sample because of how oil products will make gold float unless they are heavy nuggets.

I loaded up the samples and headed back to Dawson so that I would not have to be in a hurry panning them out. There were two fiberglass farm feed bags wound at the top with a hay wire twist. A very unique method that insured the fact I had the right bags. The first bag I opened had about two shovels of gravel in it, and when I panned it there was lots of vegetable oil floating in the pan, which told me the sample was taken at the top of the ground as soon as he had reached gravel.

I started to get excited; the bottom of the first pan

was covered with gold, way too many colors to count. I wound up with two ounces from that first bag. I opened the second bag and right away I knew I was on to something because the gravel was not typical of the existing creek bed. All the gravel in that second sample bag was the size of peanuts and as round as marbles, whereas the rocks in the existing creek were sharp and jagged.

Her step dad had discovered quite by accident, an ancient river channel, which is common in the area, and it's what made Dawson famous in the first place. There were four ounces of gold in the two shovels of material, and there were nuggets that I could pick up with my fingers.

He had said that the hole he dozed out was only five feet deep. I instantly went and found a phone and called Lizzie's step dad again, and asked him again where he had dug the hole that his samples had come from. He told me the same story on three different phone calls, and I spent the whole summer with Lizzie and my eighteen year old daughter Michelle looking for the "Hole" but we never found it, and eventually had to give up because of deteriorating fall weather.

Apparently when the flood had happened the previous October, it had changed the course of the creek and washed all the gravel away from, or back into the hole. For whatever reason we never found it, and it is still there--- somewhere---waiting for some miner born under a lucky sign. Apparently I was not born so lucky.

We saw many gold miners' strike it rich that summer, one minute they couldn't get credit at the grocery store, and the next day they were able to buy a chain of stores.

Because Dawson City is currently a tourist center for the Klondike, there are about 20 roadhouses and each one has a bar, a place to eat, and lodging.

In the old days if they could get a miner fresh from the "Diggings" (a slang term for his claim) to come in the front door, then he had no reason to leave until he was flat broke.

Each one of the roadhouses presently employs from 10 to 30 people, and about 99 % are women. It is the only place I have ever been where a beautiful girl walked up to Liz in front of me, and asked her if she could borrow or rent me for sex for an hour. She was dead serious.

That got me to thinking, all those girls and no local men, I saw an opportunity there, but I never got the nerve to say anything to Liz about it…. Probably a good thing. I have to truthfully say that Dawson is the only place I have ever been where women were sexually aggressive to the point of scaring me.

One popular story of Dawson City's early days were of a man that decided to get rich by going to Seattle and bringing back a dogsled load of eggs. Now eggs in Dawson at that time went for ten dollars and egg when they were available. He took presold a third of the eggs for four thousand dollars. When he arrived back in town at Christmas time with the frozen eggs all of the towns people gathered round to get the ones they had paid for. When all of the eggs were thawed out they had little chickens in them in various stages of development…..They were fresh when he had gotten them, but were stored on the boat on the trip to Skagway in the engine room. The temperature was to warm and all of the eggs started the hatching process. Excuses did not matter. The good people of Dawson promptly hung the enterprising man from the nearest cabin lodge pole. When I think of all that poor fellow went through to get to Seattle and bring back that load of eggs on a twelve foot freight sled through unbroken deep snow over the Chilacoot Trail…a trip of about five hundred miles cross country…well I just don't think it was fair.

While we were there, Lizzie and I got to drinking Tequila one night, and a local charter boat captain challenged Liz to a "Sour Toe Cocktail" award certificate. Now that is a drink that originated during the gold rush era. It seems a miner came in to town one day and his big toe was frozen hard as a rock, and when the Dr. thawed it out he had to amputate it. This was all done in the Klondike Roadhouse and he naturally put the toe in a glass of whisky and sat it on a shelf behind the bar to show the new comers what can happen if they did not take care of their feet.

One day a fellow came in and asked for a drink of whiskey, the bartender had to refuse because they were temporarily out. The man spied the glass with the amputated toe in it and asked to see it. The bartender handed him the glass with the toe and the man promptly tipped the glass up and drank the whiskey. Winters are long in the north and it was not long before the same miner became too drunk again one night, and not only did he drink the whisky but also ate the toe. This time there was no excuse, because they had lots of whiskey behind the bar and only the drunken man knows why he chose to eat it. Winters are long, dark and cold and the men that stayed over in Dawson found their entertainment any way they could.

Over the years since, if you can drink the whiskey out of the glass the bartender gives you a certificate called the "Sour Toe Award".

Since its inception they have had to order numerous amputated toes from some of the larger hospitals in Edmonton to keep the tradition alive because men being men would often get to drunk and eat the toe to prove that their testosterone outweighed their brain matter . And Liz not being one to shirk a challenge got a little too tipsy one night, and drank the whiskey from the glass with a toe in it. She got her certificate, but being the lady, did not eat the toe. Thank God!!! She tried and tried to get me drunk enough to get my certificate......I can't get that drunk!

Liz and I watched elderly, rich tourist ladies adorned with all their fifth avenue finery, have one too many drinks and line up to drink the cocktail, where as their male counterparts were not nearly so eager. Just goes to show females cannot resist a challenge.

Our summer in Dawson and the Klondike area was exciting and adventurous. Liz got a surge of adrenaline every time a Royale Canadian Mounted Police came in to her café, because she was working without a visa, and feared being deported or worse.

I roamed the country side just exploring and prospecting, and I learned to appreciate how hard the original miners worked to extract their gold out of the permanently frozen ground.

We left the land of golden dreams, and came back to Alaska in the fall of that same year, but our memories are burned in our minds forever......

Flying with Paul

My favorite night time dreams of flying airplanes came to an end the day my son Paul turned 16 years old. He came home that afternoon from the airstrip where he worked part time, and said, "Dad, do you remember making the promise to me, that you would let me take you up flying when I soloed?"

"Why yes son, I do." I said this thinking that was still years away, and that I would surely be in my grave by then, dead from old age.

He said, "Let's go down to the airstrip because I soloed today--- we are going flying--- I have the 170 reserved."

Well fear went through me like a hurricane does the Florida Keys. My legs went weak and my heart stopped for a full five minutes. My day to die in a plane crash! The fire that drove my fantasies, and favorite dreams would be the nightmare that ended my life.

The three mile drive to the airstrip went by way to fast. I was talking a hundred miles an hour, coming up with first one excuse then another why this just wasn't a good day for me to go flying. Paul never said a word, he just grinned, and kept driving.

It took me a good long while to get from the car to the little plane. I walked the short distance on legs of rubber, trying to figure out how to get out of this terrible mistake. I even gave considerable thought to faking a heart attack. Paul's mind was made up though, and no amount of crying or excuses worked, and finally we arrived at the airstrip. I walked around the plane just like I had seen many pilots do, only I walked around it about fifteen times inspecting the aircraft for the slightest imperfection. I grabbed the prop and gave it a yank, I looked at the wing strut bolts, and tugged on the rear flapper that makes it go up or down, then jerked on the rudder flapper thingy that turns the plane, and finally my son ran out of patience, and said, "Dad I only had this plane rented for a hour." ... "Are you a man or a mouse?" Then he gave that disarming grin of his, and right then I knew I was doomed.

When I finally slid into the front seat of the 170 next to him, I was shaking so violently that when he pulled the throttle wide open to take off, my teeth were rattling so loud in my head that I couldn't hear the roar of the engine.

After we had gotten air born, I got to thinking, (which is a mistake for me to do in an airplane) that since we were going to crash and burn when we landed, I might as well enjoy my last hour on this earth. So I said, "Son, let old Dad fly a while." It was my last request so to speak. It had two steering controls so I just took the wheel away from him and started flying and doing all the things I had done in my night time dreams.

I had had some experience flying with "Old Ron" in his piper Clipper. He had given me the controls on numerous occasions, and said I was a natural at it. But he kept a strict watch for anything that I might do to endanger us, and lectured constantly to the point that I couldn't enjoy flying the airplane.

But once at the controls of the 170, not only did I match the dreaming fantasy, I surpassed it by far, I climbed, I dove, and I flew at tree top height, I banked and barrel rolled the little Cessna with a freedom that only one that has experienced it can understand.

I literally scared that kid of mine speechless, and when I finally gave him back the controls he was as white as the paper I am typing on.

To my surprise he came in on the landing approach like a veteran bush pilot. I did not feel, even the slightest bump when the wheels touched the ground, and as we taxied in to a stop, he looked at me with that quizzical blank stare, like someone who had just cheated death, and lived to tell about it. All I could think of to say was---"Now you know how I felt, teaching you how to drive a car."

Hunting and Fishing Stories

A homestead in the middle of Alaska was a wonderful place for a teenage kid to grow up in the early years of statehood, the game was plentiful, and we were in the thick of it. I can still remember that first summer with all the new smells and sounds that were so foreign to Oklahoma where we were from.

Just before dark when the mist formed down by the creek, we would watch the moose appear seemingly from nowhere to feed on the tender grasses that grew there. I would set and watch those moose until it got too dark to see almost every night.

Grizzly bears would eat the tar paper off the edge of the roof of the house we built on the bank of the Chacock River, and it was sixteen feet from the ground. We never saw one do it, but huge bear tracks were left as evidence, and the roof had claw marks where they had somehow reached it. Wolves and coyotes ran across the little clearing in front of our garden at all hours of the day, and we listened to the lonely songs of the loons as they floated up from the misty ponds down by the river. There were lots of moose, and the spruce chickens were thick as the fleas on a dogs back in Oklahoma. I spent hundreds of hours watching and studying the wild life on our homestead and learned their habits. I had an extremely sensitive nose and could smell the difference between big game animals. I know that is hard to believe but it's true. I learned to track moose through the muskeg or timber, summer or winter, I could gut, skin, and quarter a moose in forty five minutes by the time I was fourteen. I don't think that there was any place on earth as pristine as our homestead as far as wildlife went.

My grandpaw, Haskell Alma Adkins came north with us, and brought with him one hundred thousand rounds of war surplus 30 cal carbine ammunition, and two 30 caliber carbines with lots of 30 round clips, as well as an M-1 Garand 30-06 with approximately 5,000 rounds for it and a 30.06 Springfield . He gave me the Springfield and one carbine, and my brother Daryle a carbine. It took us a year and a half to run out of ammo for the carbines. The next time he went south, he brought up much more surplus ammo for both guns. When you shoot that much ammunition, you get very accurate, especially for teenage boys that at their maximum learning curve. I loved the steel jacketed surplus ammo because it made the same size hole coming out as it did going in, which in itself saved excess damage to meat, and made the need for accuracy much greater.

My dad was not a hunter and never killed a moose that I know of. I provided all of the meat we consumed until I left home. I only know of one bull that my brother Daryle shot at, but it was my shot that brought it down. Daryle had gotten 'buck fever' and shot his horns all to hell with the M1 Garand 30-06, ruining a nice rack. After we were grown and he had a family to feed, he took many moose and was a deadly accurate shot, which helped him in Viet Nam to survive.

We wore out both of our carbines, and I almost wore out the Springfield. We practiced every known shooting position and target size. I also owned a .22 Winchester and went through countless bricks of that ammo shooting the empty casings that I would line up on a log thirty feet away. That is all we did; roam the countryside and shoot, shoot, shoot. We would spend hours taking turns throwing river rocks in the air for each other to shoot at when the sawmill was broken down and we had spare time.

That was our only pastime pleasure from the hard work of a homesteader in the early 60's, where everything we did was done by hand the hard way.

I never wanted to waste any of the meat on spruce chickens so I shot their heads off with the .30 caliber carbine. The moose I shot with the 30.06. I don't think you can take more than three steps on that whole one hundred and sixty acres without stepping on a spent bullet after we had been there four years.

I have had some fancy rifles in my life of every caliber you can think of, and some with scopes that cost more than most rifles, but to tell the truth, I was never more accurate than when shooting those world war two bolt action weapons with the ramp peep sights. I think those were the most accurate rifles ever made.

I think my folks let us shoot so much because my mother was terrified of being eaten by a huge grizzly, and it caused her to have nightmares that first year. It also it told her where we were, what we were doing, and that no bear was going to sneak up on us. Besides she was tired of churning butter from goats milk by hand, storing it in a gallon jug, and then having the grizzly's come and steal it out of our refrigerator, which was the ice cold spring just below the house. I never could figure out how a bear could smell butter in a sealed glass jar in the bottom of that spring, but they did. The first two years on that homestead, we tried raising pigs and goats. The grizzly bears ate them all.

It is now about to turn 2013 and after all these years I thought it about time to relate some of my more memorable fishing, and hunting trip stories. I have had funny and strange things happen that I cannot understand or begin to explain. I guess what I am saying is that I got tuned in, whether from exposure to all of the wild life, or the almost half breed Cherokee Indian blood in me, or possibly both. I have sat around many hunting camp fires, and listened to many hunters talk, and have never heard stories that equal some of mine for uniqueness.

The Longest Shot

I went to the Denali country in October of 1965 with my brother in law from my first wife to get a caribou; we drove up there in his 1958 Chevy sedan. Back in those days we didn't own any camping gear and needed to get a caribou the minute we got to where they were. We were really meat hungry and both of us had kids to feed. In 1965 there was no oil money, and times were tough, people basically lived off of wild game and fish for quality protein. The alternative was macaroni and cheese or hamburger helper. I had learned to hate both with an unequaled passion.

We had driven to Paxon and then west down the Denali highway but didn't see anything. Miles and miles of tundra with not one living thing to see, to say that it was disheartening was putting it mildly.

It was getting dark when we finally spotted about twenty head running parallel to the road but a long ways off. I said stop the car I'll get us one right here, and my brother in law just laughed and said, "I'll stop but that's way too far to hit anything. I jumped out and raised the ramp sight on the old 06 to a thousand yards, led the last trailing caribou about ten yards, elevated some more using Kentucky windage, and pulled the trigger. It seemed like it took forever for the bullet to get there, but when it did the caribou dropped dead, shot straight through the heart. We started walking and the snow was knee deep, but I stepped off fifteen hundred steps, and I honestly believe I was taking one yard steps. We were half the night getting all that meat back to the road.

Fishing Derby at Silver King Lodge

Catching a King Salmon on light weight gear with fresh salmon eggs is an art that seems to be learned only by people that are patient and diligent. First thing you need is a long limber fly rod with the right kind of leader that goes transparent in the water and a barbed J hook with a half inch shank and the line run through the eye and tied with a running knot down below the barbs. That way you have a loop to put the eggs in and it cinches them up tight. It is the only way to keep them on the hook. We would put a very small split shot on the line about a foot above the hook and then cast upstream about a forty five degree angle keeping the slack out of the line as it floated down the creek. If you felt a slight bump…set the hook and you had a nice female king that would weigh from thirty to fifty pounds.

Hours of watching the habits of kings from our little bridge over the Chacok had taught us that the females would pick up the eggs very gently, and then take them to a slower part of the creek and spit them out. It was nature's way of insuring the survival of the species, just like the protective instinct of a mother grabbing her child before he runs out in traffic.

We were walking home from the lower Anchor River

one day from a very successful fishing trip with six kings strung by the mouth on a long pole, and decided to stop at our river to gut the fish. I would carry one end of the pole on my shoulder, and my brother had the other end on his shoulder. The six kings had a rough weight of one hundred and eighty pounds, and not wanting to carry the extra weight, I started throwing the eggs back in the water to feed the kings I saw laying just under the bridge that I had thought up to that time ate them as food. I saw them pick them up in their mouth, but when I kept watching, they swam over to the slower water and spit them out. I could see that they were very, very gentle in the process from start to finish. I had learned their secret right there.

From that day forward until they changed the regulations forcing everyone to use a single un-baited hook, (which meant lures.) no one could out fish me or my brother. We could walk up to the river, push people out of the way and catch a king within a few minutes. They could see that we were using eggs so they would go buy some from the lodge, and put them on the hook that had a lure attached, but they didn't know how to use the eggs right, and never caught fish.

With the long limber fly rod you could feel the fish pick the eggs up. It was an ever so slight bump, like the weight might be bouncing on the bottom. Only thing was the weight we used just offset the floatation of the eggs and they floated just under the surface never touching the bottom.

We never had any money back then, and I had found the base of my fly rod on the river bank the first year I fished there. It was made out of bamboo and I never did know who made it, there was no writing on it. Then one day I found a green fiberglass upper part that someone had broken the base of and threw away. I put the two together and became a local legend when it came to catching fish. Men with rigs that cost many hundreds of dollars would look my fishing equipment, and feel sorry for the poor kid that couldn't afford a decent fishing pole, until they watched me pull big kings right out from under them. They would walk off mumbling to themselves.

The first year that the Silver King Lodge held the derby, my brother won it with a smaller fish than I had caught the first week. Mine was fatter and longer so I griped, and griped about it. He took the new spin casting outfit, and went back to fishing with a big smile on his face. The next week he won again, and again with a smaller fish than the one I turned in for the week. This time he had a T-bone dinner. The very next week he put his fish up on the weigh table, and the twenty six inch male king salmon weighed forty pounds, a fish that should have only weighed about twenty or twenty five pounds. The guy weighing the fish picked it up and dropped it over on the gutting table.........we all heard this crunching sound, and rocks rolled out of its mouth. He took off running as fast as he could laughing his head off.

Every spring when the king salmon started to move into the Anchor River my brothers, and I would stop the homestead work to go fishing, because as we so arguably stated, we needed the fish for the following winter to survive. So the month of May and June we were free of the never ending work on the homestead. We would camp on the river and only go home to take the fish.

My brothers and I became king salmon fishing experts. We would snag a female king early in the season, and harvest her eggs. I would get a metal coffee can, cut two slices about three inches long and an inch apart, then put a layer of borax soap in the bottom, then a layer of fresh eggs cut into two inch sections, then another layer of borax, and so on until the can was full. It cured the eggs, and kept them from going bad as well as toughing the up which helped them to stay on the hook. Then we would run our belts through the slices we made in the coffee can so that we had the eggs right there on our side within easy reach. We didn't have to wade out of the river to get more bait…I never saw anyone but us do that, but it worked very well.

The Surprised Moose

I was fourteen and we were still living on the homestead when I decided to get us a moose one fall.

I headed out towards the closest homesteader five miles away, that way I could eat lunch with them and have the strength to get home, besides I liked the popcorn that they always made when I would show up for a visit. I didn't see anything on the way over and the salmon patty sandwiches were delicious as was the popcorn afterward.

When I left their house I hadn't went a mile when I came across a huge bull track. The adrenaline started pumping and I got on his trail like a Blood hound after a chicken bone. A couple of hours later I knew I was getting closer but I felt like I was making too much noise, so I stopped and took my boots off. I tied the shoe strings together and threw them over my shoulder and took off on a run with nothing but my socks on my feet making no noise at all.

The Bull Moose was traveling down a well worn game trail on a ridge and he was making good time. I threw it in high gear and ran pretty fast but watching the trail to make sure he didn't leave it at some point and head for the river again.

There I was running as hard as I could go while still

being quiet, I had my head down watching his tracks with my rifle loaded and off safety. I was determined to get this moose and the usual stalking and tracking had not produced results. I stretched out my stride and kept this up for thirty minutes when I suddenly rounded a huge old growth birch tree and hit the moose right square in the ass and bounced off. Now a moose is generally about seven feet tall at the shoulder and the sight of him just before I made contact sent my heart up into my throat. But it didn't scare me as bad as it did that moose because my split second shot of adrenaline caused me to pull the trigger, and the gun went off. Together with me bouncing off his testicles (which by the way hit me squarely in the nose) and the sound of the gun going off made him dig a trench six inches deep, and a foot long with his hind feet when he jumped straight up in the air, and took off faster than I have ever seen a moose run. Needless to say, I gave up right then on that moose because I doubt he quit running until way past dark.

The 'Snogo"

In October of 1970, I was twenty three years old and in the best shape of my life. I had been married for four years and already had a wife, a son, and a new daughter to feed. I hated to go out on the oil rig camp jobs, and stay the long hitches to make money; then give it to the grocery stores for meat that was of less quality than I could get by hunting. So I bought a snow machine. They had not been out long but this one was blue and white with a single cylinder engine, it was called a "Star Craft." On a hard packed trail where there were no hills they were great, but there was a lot of room for technological advancement in those first ones, and many companies went out of business because the machines they were building were just plain no good. Such was the Star Craft as far as I am concerned..

I answered an ad in the news paper, and when I went to pick it up the guy pulled the crank rope once and it took off and purred like a kitten. I don't remember what I gave for it but it was a lot back then and it was state of the art.

I loaded up the snogo along with my gear and took off for "Gun Sight Mountain Lodge" this was a lodge that catered to caribou hunters for their winter business. They had a hunter's bunk house that would hold about fifty hunters, and for ten dollars a night you could sleep warm, then walk over to their restaurant, eat a hearty breakfast for five dollars, then go hunting from there on snow machines. They even had snow machine mechanics, and a shop that always seemed full of machines being worked on.

The limit back then was three caribou, and the "Nelchina Herd" migrated right through there. Lots of hunters simply waited in the bar or restaurant until they spotted them crossing the highway, and then ran out and shot their animals. That was way too easy for me, and not nearly adventurous enough, I felt compelled to work hard for my meat.

I proudly unloaded my snogo for the trip out early the next morning while the road hunters eyed me with envy. I have always had this problem of wanting to go where there were no other hunters, way past the end of the trail, and it has plagued me all of my life on every single hunt I ever went on. My brother Steve is the same way which made us compatible hunting partners being cursed like that.

My plan was to run in there with my nearly new machine and shoot three caribou, process them and hang the meat, then make three trips hauling the meat out to my truck. The only problem with that plan was the temperature. It was

42 below 0 and it took me hours to get the thing started. I don't think they tested that particular machine in extreme temps. When I finally got it running after putting a makeshift hose on my truck's exhaust pipe, and sticking it in the cowling to warm the engine up so that it would start, I finally got it running. I climbed on with my rifle and a snack lunch which I bought at the lodge after a nice hot breakfast of ham and eggs.

I gave it the gas and nothing happened except a huge cloud of smoke as I burned the drive belt nearly up. A fellow walking by told me that I had to lay it over on its side, and turn the rubber track for five minutes to limber it up before I rode it, then ride it around the parking lot for a while before I took off to the back country. Well I did that and by the time I left the parking lot I only had two hours of daylight left so I rode like a demon possessed to get back to where I had heard that the caribou were that day.

When I went past the last hunter I saw that he was gutting a caribou, so I stopped to talk to him. When I asked where the caribou were, he told me they were just over the hill. Now caribou were designed to travel fast in all kinds of terrain, they need raw speed to outrun wolves and bears in both deep winter snow, and the wet swampy bogs of summer.

Five miles, and many steep hills later, I saw my first woodland caribou, and it was a big bull with a set of horns that dwarfed the size of his body. In my eagerness to get back beyond all hunters, I had traveled passed the well packed trail and was in fresh deep snow. It did not take long to learn that when I needed to stop, I would make a circle and stop on my own trail, otherwise it was push and push to get it going again. In the excitement of seeing the animal I stopped in fresh snow. I shot that one and decided I wouldn't shoot any more until I got that one out to the car. Damn good idea! I tried to take off, and the track just spun digging the machine down a foot before I could get off the throttle. After heaving and tugging, I finally got the machine onto the trail I stomped out to the caribou, and got the snogo over to the animal.

I started to skin and gut the caribou but the heavy hide froze solid the minute I made a cut. I decided I had better tie a rope onto the horns and skid it out to the road in one piece. I had broken fresh snow for the last few miles and it was hip deep.

I took off and when I came to the end of the rope, the caribou moved about ten feet and I spun out, the track dug a hole straight down, and I was stuck. I got off and untied the rope and lifted the back end out of the hole, then I had to lift the front end out, then I would get the machine moving again and make a loop around on fresh snow and wind up beside my caribou. I would tie the rope on and take off as hard as it would run. The blue smoke would get thick as I burned the belt trying to pull that big animal. I could go about ten feet; sometimes if I was lucky I would make it twenty or thirty feet, and then repeat the process all over again. In the deep snow I would push the snow machine and the caribou as far as I could or the smoke would get to thick to see. To this day I don't know how that drive belt stayed together.

It was daylight the next morning when I finally pulled the caribou onto the hard trail left by hundreds of snow machines. It was a good thing because the drive belt looked like a shoe string, and it was an inch and a quarter wide when I had left the lodge.

It only took twenty minutes to get to the road from that point, and I was wore out mentally and physically. That was the longest five miles I have ever been in my life, and as soon as I had the animal tied on top of the car I went into the bunk house and slept for sixteen straight hours.

The next morning after two breakfasts and three pots of coffee, I went out to start the car, and someone had cut the head off of my caribou for its huge set of horns. I was mad clean to the bone and went back in the lodge, and offered to whip everyone in the building just so that I might get the guilty party.

When I pulled out of the lodge parking lot I began to see dead caribou gut piles all over the side of the highway. The whole Nelchina herd had moved through in the day light while I was pushing that snow machine up and down hills, and the road hunters had all gotten their limits right there in sight of the lodge.

When I finally got home the water was frozen in our house and my first wife was furious with me for staying three days on a "one day hunt" as I had promised. It was years after that before anyone could even talk to me about snow machines.

RB & Bud's First Hunt

My first wife's cousins, Bud and RB started hunting with me in about 1975. Bud was the oldest and was pretty quiet, never doubting anything I said I could do. He was old enough to always wait and see before he spoke. RB the baby brother on the other hand, was brash, quick tempered, quick to argue, very competitive, and extremely pickable, at least to me he was because I was not afraid of him the way most of our buddies were and I did pick on him unmercifully.

We were all in our late twenties by then and the first hunting trip I took them on was to mile three on the Talkeetna cut off, a road called Yoder Road named after a homesteader there.

We had started drinking beer when we left

Anchorage, and was in bad need of a pee stop when we turned off the highway. RB was fun to pick on and I did it constantly, he had a bladder the size of a thimble and was always the first one to start hollering to stop and pee. The last ten or so miles before we would stop, we would start talking about running water, and how the sounds of water falls were like the tinkle of water dripping out of a can and hitting a rock, then just before we would stop I would cut a beer can in half (There was always beer) and slowly pour some beer into the can I had cut in half, letting it tinkle, sometimes I would waste a whole beer doing that to him...well RB was impressionable to the max, and would start cussing us something terrible. He would be screaming at us by the time we finally stopped. It would go something like this...."You m***** F****** do this to me every time and I'm always the one in the middle, I'm driving from now on , and I'm going to piss in both of your sleeping bags, pull this m***** F***** over before I pull my johnson out and piss all over both of you right now." Of course he never did any of the things he threatened but I guess it made him feel better to say it.

We had just pulled off the highway and around the first turn on Yoder road when I stopped and said, "RB now get out of here and empty that thimble bladder of yours." He bailed out and started irrigating the back tire like a dog, just to get even with me since it was my truck. Of course he finished first and grabbed his old colt .45 and looked around for something to shoot at. Bud said still pissing said, "shoot that squirrel in the top of that tree over across the road there," and pointed to the tree.

You can't do that now, because it's wall to wall houses from the Y junction to Talkeetna, but back then there were only about three houses on the entire thirteen mile road, and RB started shooting at that poor squirrel. He didn't come anywhere close to hitting the thing, and finally Bud got his .357 Ruger frontier model out and started shooting, then our old buddy Bruce got his .44 magnum out and started shooting. The squirrel was safe and sound and never moved except to chatter at us. Actually I think he was laughing at them. Finally after what seemed like thirty minutes and lots of ammo later, Bud said, "Show em how is done Mel." I had strapped on my .44 Ruger Blackhawk and was just watching. They all turned to look at me, so I fast drew and shot from the hip. Down came the dead squirrel. I lifted the end of the barrel to my lips like I had seen the cowboys do in the movies do, and blew the smoke away, then holstered my pistol, and got back in the truck. RB was screaming red faced with rage, "I'll give you a hundred dollars if you can do that again." Bud finally said, "I don't think he can resurrect that squirrel, bro." Bruce just looked at me with admiration. Of course it was shit house luck but they never knew that for sure and always wondered about it in the coming years.

When we got to the end of Yoder road we stopped, and spent the night in the camper since it was too late to go on up the trail, and it had started to rain. The next morning when we all climbed out I looked at Bud and asked him what was wrong with him. His belly looked pregnant…huge… to the point I worried about him, so I told him we might ought to go back to the hospital and see what was wrong……about that time he started farting and let the longest fart I have ever heard in my life, and with all the bush jobs I have worked in my career, I have heard some duzies. When he finally stopped after a full minute or so he looked so skinny that it was pitiful. We all laughed so hard our sides hurt.

After breakfast we loaded our camp on the "Dynamite" which is a four wheel drive articulated swamp buggy, and headed for the end of the trail, which at that time was about five miles. We set up camp, and still had some daylight left. I put Bud on a good place on the trail, and told him to keep quiet and there would be a big bull coming right by him before sundown. I said if you are still, he will walk within ten feet of you, so hold your fire until he gets close enough that you are sure you can hit him. I then left to find a spot for Bruce and RB. Now I know that there is no way in hell that RB and Bruce can be quiet so I found a place that looked out over a mile of swamp so that they would have at least a fighting chance to see something.

I went back to camp and finished setting it up, then I cooked supper for the bunch. When the meal was prepared, I went out to retrieve Bud. Before I got to where he was I could hear him snoring, then I saw the bull moose tracks right over the track I had made leaving…..yes they went right by Bud… within ten feet of him while he was snoring. I had to actually yell at him to get him awake.

"How come you didn't shoot that monster bull that walked by here a little while ago?" I asked. "Were you sleeping?"

He opened his eyes and replied, "I was not; I was just lying here resting. Damn my throat is sore; I think I'm coming down with something. Besides I'm not RB and you can't pull that crap on me, there aint been any moose walk by here." I showed him the tracks in the soft damp dirt on top of our earlier foot prints, and he got a dumbfounded look on his face. He stood there looking dumbfounded trying to put all the pieces together in his foggy, freshly awoke mind.

"If you tell the boys about this I won't ever forgive you, and…and, I will get even with you somehow if you do!" he said it in the most menacing voice he could come up with.

The minute we got back to camp I told all of them about the moose walking by Bud while he was snoring, and I had to take RB and Bruce down the trail so that they could see for themselves. They had to know beyond a shadow of a doubt, because they would tease him all winter in the paint and body shop they owned and operated in Anchorage, and would tell anyone that got into a conversation about hunting, that story. Poor Bud, there was just too much evidence to deny it…but it was just too good to keep to myself.

RB's Out House

The next hunting season I took them all including my brother Steve to the Denali country at mile post 60 on the Denali highway, to a trail that eventually we pushed all the way to the Big Susitna River a distance of 60 trail miles. We made camp beyond the end of the trail a half mile, and set up the tent down on a small creek.

We had taken a chainsaw with us and cut up about three cords of fire wood, all of our hunts on the Denali were ten day hunts, and we needed that much wood to last. I had gotten resourceful and creative over the years and any hunters that came by our camp, would look at us with envy. We would stack the fire wood up and form a room that we could stretch a tarp over and with a fire in the middle, it would be warm and comfy even in freezing temperatures. The ever present breeze that came over the top of the stacked firewood would take the smoke away….It was ingenious.

Now RB had to have a nice "Shitter" as he called it, and set to work the next day building one out of visqueen and willow poles. He had found a discarded piece of ¾ plywood, and used the chainsaw to make the hole for a seat. It was admired by all that saw it or used it.

The very first night after the camp was set up to our satisfaction, we were sitting around telling lies, drinking beer, and feeling way to smug about our ingenuity, when a Grizzly suddenly walked right into camp, the stacked firewood made it impossible for the bear to see us or hear us, and when RB stood up to stretch he looked right into the eyes of the Grizzly standing just across the pile of wood less than three feet away. It scared him so bad that he had nightmares, and of course I didn't help matters after that by telling made up stories about bear attacks in the Denali country. So RB started right then wanting to sleep in the back of the tent, and never taking off his colt 45…he would even take it to bed with him inside his sleeping bag.

Now you could set your watch by RB's bowels and exactly five minutes after breakfast he would have to go to his outhouse, so the next morning after the bear had walked into camp, I ate fast and grabbed my gun and took off without telling anyone where I was going. I circled the camp and took up a spot about ten feet behind the fancy outhouse he had built. That was the only place he went without his colt 45, and sure enough at exactly five minutes after breakfast I saw RB coming up the trail to his home made out house. I was not even hid that well, I just had the outhouse between the trail and him.

I almost laughed out loud at the noises he was making and when I heard a real loud grunt from him I ran up to the backside of his out house, beat on the plastic and growled really loud like a grizzly. Then I jumped to the side so I could watch. He busted through the door without opening it, and his pants were still around his ankles…he was taking little tiny steps and there was a foot long turd hanging out his butt. He was screaming, bear…bear at the top of his lungs. Needless to say I almost laughed myself to death, my sides hurt for days.

After about two hours of nonstop cussing me, he told me that he would be taking his colt to the outhouse with him, to shoot without hesitation anything that made a noise. Three days later he was sitting on his throne when we heard the loud report of his pistol. We ran to see what he had shot at. We were all thinking that a grizzly was attacking him, but when we got there he was admiring his new boot which had a 45 caliber hole just to the right of his big toe, and above his second toe at the end of the boot. His two toes had burn marks on them from the bullet as it blew the end out of his boot. He had been fiddling with the hammer still in the holster and it slipped of his thumb, causing it to fire.

I believed him when he told me that he would shoot me if I ever scared him again so I never did in all the years we hunted together until his accidental death in a ford pickup in 1985 ended his hunting trips forever.

The Moose That Called My Name

I always have had the ability to spot game long before anyone else. I don't know why, but it might be that my vision when I was younger was 13/20...I could see at 20 feet what the average person could see at 13 feet. When I was thirteen I was jumping a six volt battery from a twelve volt battery when it exploded and filled my eyes with acid. I ran blindly all the way home, a distance of a half mile so that mom could wash the acid out of my eyes. I have thought over the years that may have had something to do with my extraordinary eye sight, it probably didn't but I always thought so.

There were times when I would get frustrated trying to tell the people in my party where the moose was standing in plain sight. I would see the moose without the binoculars, "See that little meadow up at the base of that hill over there, the moose is standing next to that clump of bushes down near the bottom of that draw." When they would finally see it, they might say something like, Hell Mel, that's three miles away, and it looks like a stump to me, then the stump would move out of sight and they would say, damn you have eagle eyes.

One year at that same little camp site, we were sitting around the fire in our little firewood condo after a hard days hunting and supper was just getting done when I got this strange feeling, and an urge to walk down the creek from the camp which I couldn't resist. "Boys," I said, "Go ahead and eat without me, there's a moose calling my name right down the creek here, and I'm going to go get him."

Yeah sure, they all said in unison…your nuts, but if you want to miss supper go ahead.

I threw some biscuits I had brought along in my pocket, and grabbed my rifle and took off. A half mile from camp, I came to a small ridge that was about twenty feet high. I crept up slowly, a strange feeling of excitement and anticipation consumed me. When I topped the ridge, there not fifty feet was a huge bull moose facing me. I slowly raised my rifle, took aim and shot him right between the eyes, he reared over backwards dead. I cut his throat and gutted him, and because it was starting to get dark I headed back to camp.

When I walked into camp, they all started making fun of me… "Where's the big bull?" they would ask, "Where is the blood?"

"As soon as I eat," I said, "You guys need to be ready to go help me skin, and load it on the dynamite."

"Right!" They all said in unison, and no one made a move to do anything but drink more beer.

When I got through wolfing down some left over's, I got up and said, "I'm not kidding, come on you guys, I am serious." It wasn't until I actually started the machine that they got up and loaded the dynamite with beer, and reluctantly went with me down the game trail towards the moose.

I guess because of my past pranks on all of them, they still didn't believe I had shot a moose until we went over the little ridge and there was my moose. When I shot, the big bull reared up and went over backwards, landing between to grass clumps like a big cradle. His head and upper torso was elevated, making it the easiest moose I have ever field dressed. Gravity worked for me, and the guts slid right out between his back legs smooth as silk.

I rubbed it in and told lots of bull shit stories about how game would call my name, but in actuality it did happen from time to time. But I had them all believing I possessed a superior power that they didn't, and who knows maybe I did, at times it certainly appeared so.

Too Much Testosterone

One year on the Denali hunt, Bud and RB brought two dirt bikes and RB rode one in. Bud on the other hand had more sense, as he always did, and rode with me on the mud buggy I had built out of a 1966 dodge 4x4. I had built a bench seat way up in the air and riding up there you could see out over the brush. It made it a lot better for hunting, and Bud loved to ride up there. His bike was loaded on the back of the buggy, and RB rode his with a tow rope attached. Every time we crossed a creek his ass got wet and we could hear him cussing. We laughed and laughed till we couldn't laugh, tears were streaming down our faces; that's how funny it was. When he would ride up on the rope, he would stop, then the rope would come tight and he would have the front wheel turned, and get jerked off of it into the ice cold water, and we would hear him yelling and cussing. He never learned not to run up on the rope that whole way in. That was the funniest trip I ever took going the forty miles in to our camp.

After we had camp set up, we spent five days hunting caribou unsuccessfully. Then I ran out of cigarettes, so I smoked all of RB and Bud's cigars that they would turn loose of.

I found out a friend of mine that smoked was a few miles down the trail, so I decided to go to his camp and bum some smokes. RB wanted to go with me and suggested that we ride the dirt bikes.

We were going along pretty smoothly when we came to a deep little creek, and for some reason I made it across without any trouble, but not RB. He stalled in the middle and fell over in that freezing water fresh off of a glacier. I heard him gurgle and yell, and when I looked back he was completely submerged. Do I have to tell you how hard I laughed…. His head popped up out of the water and I could hear his teeth chattering, so I got a rope that I had brought along and tied it to my bike and then to RB's.

All this time he was standing in that waist deep water freezing his nuts off. He climbed on the bike and said hit it. I took off knowing I would have to have momentum to get him out, but what I didn't expect was that the bike got jerked right out from under him, slick as a whistle and he hit the water in a sitting position. Again I about laughed myself nearly to death and RB was so mad at me, that he cussed me for five minutes with every cuss word he knew and in a few languages I did not recognize.

Now RB is the only person on this planet that could cuss me that way, and I never took offence. First off, he weighed about one hundred and forty pounds soaking wet and he looked like a little Mexican bandito with his handle bar mustache. Funny looking is what I'm trying to say, and I just never could get mad at him no matter what he did to me. We had that kind of relationship.

We got back on the trail after an hour of trying to dry

his bike out by pulling it, we finally got it running and I took off in the lead. As soon as I got up to speed a caribou jumped in the trail in front of me. For some reason only known to God, I decided to run up on him and shoot him with my .44 pistol. Well the bike I was riding had a low range, and it was stuck in it. I opened up the throttle and gained on the caribou and at the last second before I shot.....I got a really dumb idea.....hell I would bull dog it like I used to do calves when I was a kid in Oklahoma. I put my pistol back in the holster and leaned out to grab the horns and he put on a burst of speed...I opened up the throttle wide open and caught back up to him, then leaned out again to bull dog the caribou...he put on another burst of speed. I could get almost up on him and he just kept changing gears and going faster. We came to a sharp curve, he stayed on the trail and I went out through the pucker brush, and into a large stand of willows. I had scratches all over my face, and when I got back to the trail there was RB laughing his ass off. The only thing he said was, "Man your testosterone outweighed your brain matter on that one."

The first and only time he got to laugh at me in all the years we hunted together.

False Security

We slept in tents back then that was always way too small for the number of hunters in our party, and RB insisted that he be allowed to sleep in the back of the tent as far away from the zippered door as he could get. I asked him why one day, and he said, "Cause when that bear comes in that door he will get you before he can get to me."

I laughed and called him a chicken. Many years later when we had a bigger tent, he still insisted on sleeping as far from the door as he could get, and one year after we almost fought over the only smooth place in the tent floor, which happened to be in the back of the tent. I said, "RB don't you realize that a bear don't know what or where the door is, if he wants to come in he will make his own door which ever direction he's coming from with one swipe of his claws. Of all the bear attacks you've heard of, have you ever heard of one coming through the zipper door?" The look on RB's face was priceless. He had never stopped to think about that. Not once in all those years. He started cussing me and went at it for twenty minutes, calling me every known nasty word in the human vocabulary. Finally he took a break to catch his breath and I asked him why he was cussing me and this was his answer, I have retold it so many times I remember it from heart.

"You f****** a**h***, son of a b**** m*****f******, you let me sleep back there knowing all along I was not any safer than the rest of you m****f*****a**h****. Why did you have to tell me now, you sick f****** b******. Aint you ever heard that ignorance is bliss? Im gonna sleep in the middle from now on if I have to whip every one of you m*****f******."

And he did sleep in the middle of the tent from that moment on until his last hunting trip. Again I laughed so hard that I almost peed my pants and had sore ribs most of the hunting trip.

Stretch Them Horns

One year in the mid seventies, we all arrived at the gravel pit on the Denali Highway, and started loading up the hunting buggies. By this time I had welded the front and real differentials on the old 66 dodge mud buggy, making it positive four wheel drive, then I added duals all the way around, and put dump truck chains on all four wheels. It would literally climb a tree. I had power steering, and that was the only way I could have ever steered it with the duals and the differentials being welded solid, but it put a lot of strain on the drag link and pitman arm. Anyway when we were loading up the buggies an old man came over and started talking to us. He was up from Alabama and wanted to get him a set of horns for his retirement home, and be able to show his "LODGE" buddies, and have some bull session stories to go along with it. He said we could have the meat as the horns were all he wanted.

I felt sorry for the old man for some reason, and invited him to go along with us, beside I was raising a family and could use the extra meat. I also knew it was his last great hurrah, as far as hunting in Alaska went, and I wanted to help him out and be a part of it. Usually I did not mess with road hunters at all. I told him he could ride in with us, and I would drop him off at a good vantage point I knew of that overlooked a river bottom, and we would pick him up on the way out, but it was up to him to get his moose and do all the meat packing back up to the trail.

We dropped him off at the spot, and we went on in to the end of the trail. We were all successful in our hunt that year, and every one had gotten their caribou and moose. That meant lots of trips back and forth hauling the meat out. It was a picture perfect year for temperature on hanging meat, it cured and crusted beautifully.

On the first trip out we stopped by the old man's camp, and sure enough, he had a young bull hanging on the meat rack. Some younger hunters had come by and saw him struggling with the quartered meat, trying to get it hung on the meat rack that had been there since our bunch had put it up many years before. They stopped and helped him, and probably saved him a heart attack.

I asked him where the horns were and he told me they were still down at the gut pile, and that he was too wore out to get them back up the ridge after he had packed the meat out by himself.

I knew the law said that the horns were to be kept as proof of sex by the fish and game, so I drove my buggy down and retrieved them. They looked awfully small to me, the limit was thirty six inches, so as soon as I got back up the ridge I got out a tape measure, and sure enough the horns were twenty nine and a half inches wide. I asked him if he knew that it was an illegal moose he had shot. He told me that he thought for sure it had three brow tines on one side which would have made it legal. He also told me that it had been raining and his glasses were fogging up on him. We believed him and I told him about my dad once in Colorado, stretching deer horns. Why I don't know but he did it and told us about it, in case us kids ever had to do that we would know how.

I told the old man what I had seen my father do but that it was against the law, but he decided to do it anyway, and cut the 2x4 the right length and made him some wedges. Every twenty four hours he would add a wedge until it measured thirty eight inches, then when he took the last wedge out as the fish and game helicopter landed, his horns came back to thirty six inches.

We went on our way making trips, hauling meat from our camp. The morning of our last trip, as we got to the old man's camp, the helicopter landed, and a fish and game officer walked up to check licenses. He looked at the horns and got his tape measure out and measured the width of the horns. They measured thirty six inches exactly. He would look at the horns and then look at the old man. The skull plate was almost touching on the underneath side. He finally asked the old man point blank if he had stretched the horns....

"Of course not!" was his reply.

"Well I'll bet that was one funny looking moose," The officer said, "But it measures right so there is nothing I can do about it since I didn't catch you with that 2x4 in use," and he pointed at the board the old man had used to stretch them with. "You know it's a twenty five hundred dollar fine for doing that don't you?" he asked, looking at the old man and smiling.

Normally fish and game officers don't have any sympathy for rule breakers, none, zip, nada, but I think he found the same compassion for the old man that I did, and decided to let him go. The skull plate touching was a dead give away, and he had the old fellow dead to rights.

We loaded up his moose, and took him and his horns to the gravel pit with stories to tell for the rest of his life about his great Alaskan moose hunt. I have never condoned the illegal taking of wild life but I was glad that I helped make it happen for him.

First Jump up Shot

We had pushed the trail way on back before RB got killed, and on his last hunting trip we set up camp on a high ridge so that we could stay in camp, drink beer, and hunt at the same time.

Also by this time RB and Bud had built a buggy of their own by using a 1979 chevy half ton 4x4 pickup with DC-3 airplane tires. It sure set it up in the air, and they needed a ladder to climb in, but it was a good rig. RB told me he needed a truck to haul his camp in. That consisted of a full bed load of beer with this huge ten man military tent and generator along with a string of twenty lights. Then he had to make a trip to haul in the food and more beer. We all camped together for the company, and the beer drinking BS sessions that took place in the evenings around the campfire.

We had just got through eating breakfast one morning after not seeing anything for two days of hunting, and I told them that if I saw a caribou he would get shot... even if I had to learn to fly.

RB said, "Well I'd like to see that, you Daniel Boone son of a bitch." Because by this time he was afraid to doubt me but he couldn't help it, it was just his nature, and he always had this competition thing going on with me. He hated to be wrong, oh how he hated being wrong or outdone.

At that time the tundra willows were about shoulder high and all you could ever see was the caribou's horns above the brush and usually just out of range. The terrain from our camp was uphill in back of us, and our view was panoramic. I stood up to stretch, and then threw my plate down and grabbed my rifle. I took off through the pucker brush on a dead run. I had seen a set of horns that had to be the largest I had ever seen on a caribou going in a diagonal direction away from me. I knew I could never catch up to him but if I got lucky...I might get a shot.....I was desperate to get some meat. Well I'm running as quiet and as fast as I could and thinking all the time... thinking, and thinking about how I was going to pull this off with all the guys at the camp that had a bird's eye view of the whole shebang. I had a reputation to uphold!

All of a sudden the answer presented itself, I came around a tall bunch of brush and there was a huge rock with a slope that was from ground up... to just about the height of the bushes, but still concealed from them, so I slid my rifle safety off and ready to fire, and ran up the rock and jumped as high as I could, shouldered the rifle and shot. Down went the caribou. When I got back to the camp they all looked at me with strange, strange looks on their faces. They waited patiently for me to speak and I finally said, "Told you I would get a caribou today even if I had to fly." .....dead silence.....no one said a word.

When I drove the machine up to load the caribou, I intentionally avoided the place where the rock was, and they never saw it.

I laughed for years every time I think about that, and wonder what really went through their minds, because I never told them what happened with the rock. I never thought that I was all that lucky, and just figured I was that good of a shot. Sounds awful presumptuous I know, but it's what I think.

Back in Anchorage at Bud and RB's body and paint shop, I was the local hero when it came to hunting....a hunting God... they even put a picture of me on the wall by the phone and underneath was the caption, "The Great White Hunter." I loved it dearly, and never missed an opportunity to build on my reputation with BS or trickery. There was always more beer drinking and bull sessions than work sitting around the heater in the winter time with all of our old cronies, but not one single time did any one of them ever bring up the fact that I suddenly appeared in the air; my feet three feet higher than the six foot bushes surrounding the dead caribou.

The Bull Moose That Wouldn't Die

I never missed a shot at game in my life except for two times, once was when my brother Steve and I extended the trail to the big Sue River, a total of sixty trail miles from the gravel pit where all of our trips started from . That last ridge we crossed before the river was quite a thing to see. We looked down into a sloping little valley and there were moose everywhere. Big horns shinning in the sunlight in any direction we looked, and no cows in sight.

We picked out two of the biggest that were standing together way off to one side in a little meadow, at what looked to be a quarter of a mile away. We shut the old Dodge mud buggy off, grabbed our guns, and took off after them.

Now let me tell you about distance deception in the high tundra country….It's very hard to judge distance. Now days every hunter has a range finder including me, but not back then. We walked, and walked, and walked some more; that smooth looking meadow turned into a knee deep bog with little creeks that were two feet across and six feet deep. I know because I fell in one. The willow bushes were taller than we were. When we finally got to where we thought we could shoot at one, there was only one left standing there. We never did see the other one, and to this day have no idea where he went, it didn't seem like there was anyplace he could hide when we spotted them from up on that ridge.

We settled down and caught our breath, then used a grass clump to rest our rifles on, I told Steve to shoot first, and I would shoot next if he missed. The moose started running. We wanted meat first off but we wanted that huge rack as well. We had never been anything but meat hunters, but this time it was different…..we could have both.

Steve shot and missed, the bull stopped, and stood

there as if nothing in the world was wrong. He shot again, missed, shot again, missing. Finally he said that I should shoot next. I shot, missed, shot again, missed, we both started shooting and missing. Finally I told him that since the moose was deaf and dumb, that maybe we should get closer since he hadn't moved an inch or even flinched in the last fifteen minutes.

We both carried our back packs with all the ammo we needed to start a small war. We crept another hundred yards closer which cut the distance in half, and started shooting again. We shot half of our backpack full of ammo, and decided to sneak closer yet. We cut that distance in half. Again we shot and shot, but we were still missing. By this time we didn't even try to keep our voices quiet. Either we were shooting at a statue someone had put out here in the middle of nowhere or the moose was dead on his feet, and rigor mortis had set in causing him to stay standing with three boxes of 300 win mag boat tail bullets in his body from one end to the other. We aimed, and shot in front, behind, under, and over him after we got tired of shooting at his heart.

We cut that distance in half again and I swear I could almost touch him. I told Steve that if this didn't work I would run up and stab him with my knife. He shot and missed, I shot and missed, finally I just looked down the side of my barrel and pulled the trigger. Down he went.

When we got back to the camp our hunting buddies set up while we were melting down our barrels, we checked our rifles, and both of our scopes were loose, and about to fall off. Since both guns were jinxed, we sold them and bought new ones the next summer.

The Caribou That Wouldn't Die

One year Liz and I went to a gold mine to work, I would run heavy equipment and Liz would cook. The ptarmigan were on an upswing of their life cycle and were thick. The blueberries were also thick and it made the birds so sweet and good that we called it ptarmigan candy, it was that good. Every evening I would get on my 6- wheeler and go shoot a dozen, Liz would soak them in wine for a hour, and then roll them in flour and fry them. Every morning I would climb on the backhoe with my pockets full of ptarmigan and biscuits. I will never forget that time period of time we spent at the gold mine. Liz washed clothes in water which had ice in it from the glacier just up the creek from us. God that is one tough woman!

Hunting season came and I grabbed my 300 win mag. And headed out to see if I could find one; we were broken down at the mine, the owner had gone to town for parts, so we had the day to ourselves.

About the time I got to the airstrip a herd of caribou came into view on the airstrip. I picked out a nice bull with a huge rack, actually I think it was the leader of the herd. I used my 6-wheeler as a rest and took aim at him. Bang, miss, bang, miss. Oh no I thought, not a repeat of the moose with Steve so I got closer, and still missed. The old bull wandered off as unconcerned as if I wasn't even there. I followed him and got closer. Bang, miss, bang, miss. He looked to be about two hundred yards so I shot under him, then over him, then behind him, then in front of him....all misses. The old caribou would look at me, then take a few steps, and I would shoot some more. I finally ran out of bullets. Then just like in the movies a helicopter rose up from under the ridge in front of me which I never heard, and the guy yelled down at me, "You know this herd is protected don't you."

My scope was fine and I had sighted it in the day before, it was dead on. I went back to the airstrip after I retrieved some more ammo, and shot at a rock the same distance that I had shot at the old bull, and nailed the rock ever time......Did I have an angel watching out for me, and curving my bullets? Or was the old caribou bull an invincible ghost? I will never know, but I shot two boxes of shells at him, and never was shooting farther than two hundred yards. At that distance I was deadly accurate normally. I don't know.....It will always remain a mystery to me.

My second Jump Shot

The hunting season of 1982, I decided to help my brother Steve get his "Pug" ready for the hunting trip. The times were tough and we really need to hunt cheap, so I decided to go with him on his machine. When the maintenance was done and we were packed up and ready to leave, Steve's long time friend who happened to be named Steve as well showed up ready to go hunting. Normally we only wanted two men to a machine but our buddy didn't have one at the time, and we agreed he could go with us on the Pug.

The Pug was built on the same principle as the Dynamite, meaning it articulated in the middle and swiveled on the center joint. It had a box built on the back to haul your camp and game. The only problem was that it was factory built and parts were hard to find, and you could load way to much weight in the rear box for what it could safely haul.

We arrived at the gravel pit where we were met by fish and game. They told us that we couldn't leave the pit and go down the trail.

We were used to getting into camp early so that we could be assured of our same old camping spot at the end of the trail. We asked them what was going to happen and they said that at 1201am on opening day they were going to turn every one loose at the same time. A short cocky game warden smiled at us and said, "Kinda like that Oklahoma Land Rush."

We started drinking beer and continued to drink for three days while we waited. When the magic hour arrived there were sixty or seventy hunting machines loaded with drunk hunters, us included. The fish and game used a flare gun for the start, and the Oklahoma Land Rush didn't have a thing on that mad melee. All of those machines with the headlights on was something to see all strung out for a mile down the trail. They were all trying to get on the trail at the same time, running those buggies as fast as they would go. Machines would come in out of the brush where they had hidden the night before.

The first five miles were on a hard packed wide trail and people were passing each other on both sides…It was pure havoc, but fun as hell, especially when your dog drunk and can't see a thing in the dark. Our machine would run way too fast for the terrain. We passed some of the slower rigs and got passed by the faster ones. If I steered a little too far one way, it would over steer in the other direction, and I would have to slow down and get back in the trail without getting ran over. Just when I thought things were looking really good the left front tire hit a clump of grass and went left suddenly. We went air born, landed in a bog, and the tork of the engine at full throttle made the rear part spin over and dump the whole load of hunting gear in that bog. I might have avoided the grass hump but for the beer I had in each hand.

That hunting trip ended right there, It took us a full day to dig our gear out of the mud and dried and reloaded. We had to go home humiliated, and of course our buddies would not let us live it down, especially me. They never got much chance to make fun of me and when they did, they drove it in the ground.

When I got home I decided to hunt the local moose population. There were lots of big bulls in the area, and I knew I could get meat for the freezer, but the Denali hunts were a get together of hunters from all over the state that congregated every year purely for the love of the Denali tundra country. We were a close knit bunch and would do anything for a fellow hunter.

My daughter Michelle who was about thirteen at that time loved to go fishing with me, so I thought I would take her with me for a road hunt. On one of the back roads behind Montana Creek there was a place you could park, and see for a mile each direction in prime moose country. I had seen lots of tracks while I had been back there cutting winter fire wood for the wood shed, so I knew moose crossed the road early in the morning and late in the evening just before dark, going back and forth into the creek bottom.

We had been sitting there in the truck talking when a blur of movement in the rear view mirror got my attention, and I looked around and saw a bull crossing the road behind me. I grabbed the rifle and took off on the run after him. About half a mile later just when I was getting close enough for a shot, he heard me and broke into a run. Only his head and upper shoulders were visible in the tall willow brush, so in desperation I jumped up in the air and shot. I was aiming as I went up, and when I reached the crest of the jump I fired. Down he went.

I have done that jumping up and shooting at running animals two times in my life and both times I brought the animals down. Michelle wanted to help me process the moose and held the flashlight while I worked. The smell of fresh guts made her sick and she puked right there. She has been a vegetarian ever since.

I saw my brother do that jump up and shoot thing once on a caribou, that was about five hundred yards off, and running away from him. He was using a 243 and while running he jumped up and shot… the caribou dropped stone cold dead. If I had not seen it with my own eyes, I would not have believed it possible. Lucky…perhaps, but I prefer to think all of the shooting we did as kids paid off at times when we really needed it to.

I saw my brother Steve, do that same thing on one of our Denali hunts, when the monster moose I shot in the chest with a 243 just grunted and ran off. I had every intention of shooting him in the head, as the .243 was deadly accurate but lacked the knock down power for a body shot on such a large animal. For some reason known only to a higher power, at the last second I dropped the sights to his chest, which was ridiculously stupid on my part.

As with my other brother, I was on a ridge above looking down on sloping terrain, I could see the whole thing take place.

Steve chased after the moose on a dead run, every once in a while the moose would stop to see what was chasing him, and then Steve would gain a little on him. He finally must have given up on the idea of getting really close, and jumped into the air above the brush, and fired. Down went the moose, and it was the largest bodied moose I have ever had the privilege of hanging on a meat rack. It looked to me like a 75 to 100 yard shot he made that day.

I have been around lots of hunters, and asked them if they have ever heard of it being done. Not one hunter has ever told me that he has made a jump shot. Most likely because they had more sense than to even try. Like the old saying goes. "Necessity is the mother of invention." In our case in was the hunger, and necessity for meat. I don't know why three brothers raised in the woods pulled it off when it needed to be done, but I swear by all that is holy that it happened.

Out Of Bullets.

In 1968, I went to Sourdough to get some caribou, the limit was thee per person, and the season was almost year round. About two hundred hunters waited until the herd migrated across the highway, then it sounded like world war three was taking place.

I had heard on the local news in Anchorage that the caribou were crossing at Sourdough Lodge so I got in the car, picked up my brother in law, and headed up there. When we arrived at the lodge, it was already dark, and -42 was showing on the Sourdough Lodge thermometer. The generator for the lodge had shut down due to a frozen fuel line. They burned firewood for heat so the lodge was warm. The owner was trying to get it going but he was not a mechanic.

My brother in law and I both were mechanics so we decided to help him get it going. A quick check told us that the fuel line had frozen up at the tank. Actually the fuel the owner had ordered was regular diesel fuel, and it had jelled, which is a lot like frozen. It was bitter cold, and we frost bit our fingers but we thawed it out, and in a course of an hour had it up and purring like a kitten.

The owner told us that without our help, he didn't know how long it would have taken him to figure it out and get it going. He told us to bunk in the bunkhouse with the other hunters. We took him up on it and spent a warm night in that bunkhouse.

The next morning we went in to the lodge for breakfast and coffee. I remember we ate bacon and eggs with sourdough toast, and coffee. When we finished eating we went to the cash register to pay what we thought would be a token amount because of our invaluable help on the generator.

Now back then goose down, had just made its transition from pillows to coats, and it was extremely high priced, no one that I knew of could afford to wear it. Wool was the warm fabric, and it didn't do much good at -40. What I am trying to say is…. that this man was miserable while he was trying to fix that generator, freezing his ass off in that extreme temperature, and he really showed his appreciation by handing us a $220. bill for our stay at the sourdough lodge. In 1968 $220. was a hell of a lot of money. A ten dollar bill would buy all of the gas we could burn going up there and back, without shutting the engine off the whole trip. We were afraid to shut it off…it might not start in those temperatures.

I looked at my brother in law and he looked at me, and then at the guy, then he said, "f*** you, you f****** crooked f****r," then he threw a twenty dollar bill on the counter and said, " stick this up your ass for the next time it gets 40 below, and your f****** generator quits." Then we stomped out daring anyone to follow us outside. There were no cell phones back then, and no phone service that far out of anchorage. Otherwise we might not have gotten away with not paying his price.

We got in the car and headed up the highway to where the other hunters in the bunkhouse had said the caribou were crossing the road. When we arrived at the spot, there were dead caribou everywhere, people were busy processing their game, and I thought we were too late, so I grabbed my rifle and took off into the brush. I went approximately a hundred yards, when all hell broke loose behind me towards the road. I heard bullets whizzing past my ears and I sat down under a little tree and tried to be as inconspicuous as I could, not wanting to get shot.

Apparently a small herd crossed the road where we were parked and my brother in law didn't even have a gun, but a bus load of GI's from Elmendorf air force base had just arrived as I left the road. They opened up on the herd with what sounded like AR-15's on full automatic.

I hunkered down and waited for the shooting to stop…finally it did, and then I saw the caribou coming straight for me. I waited until they were going past me about ten feet away, then I shot the first two, a cow and a young bull. I was out of bullets. I had taken off so fast from the car that I had forgotten to make sure I had plenty of ammo…..a thing very unlike me.

The last caribou in line of what was left of the herd came abreast of me, stopped, and looked straight at me…..I swear…..he was asking me to finish him…he was shot to ribbons, and bleeding severely, blood was coming out of his mouth in a red foam. I got my knife out and jumped on his back and grabbed his horns, we thrashed around some but eventually because of his loss of blood I got him wrestled down, and cut his throat. Had he been a healthy bull, the outcome most likely would have been decidedly different.

Bad Mo Jo

I have always thought that one reason I had an advantage over the average hunter was the half breed Cherokee Indian blood in me that I inherited from my mother. I tried to use that advantage every time the opportunity presented itself.

The last hunt my brother Steve and I was on turned into a disaster. We each had 6-wheelers, and we loaded up for a caribou trip to the forty mile country up past Chicken close to the Canadian border. When we got to Chicken, they told us the road was closed due to heavy rains washing the road out in numerous places. So we had to wait until the next caravan would be led through by pilot car.

We set up our tent in their camp ground and had to pay dearly for that privilege, then spent the next two days exploring the hunting trails in that area, but mostly we watched it rain.

When the caravan finally pulled out there was about a hundred of us, mostly hunters, and it was a slow grind up the washed out road in steady rain.

I don't remember how long it took to make the trip but when we finally got through to the Y seven miles before the border, the state had the road blocked about a half mile before the port of entry. When we took the road past the Y to Eagle it was blocked off at the seven mile marker. Five hundred hunters were all stuck in a fourteen mile stretch of road and no caribou.

We set up our tent and spent two days watching it rain, and starring into the heavy mist until we were cross eyed looking for a stray lost caribou to no avail. We were running low on water so we decided to go to the Canadian border to fill our water jugs. When we got there the road was still blocked, and a fish and game official stopped us and would not let us through to the lodge because we were "Hunters". He made us park our truck and walk the half mile with our water jugs to the lodge. Mad is not the word for how we felt. Of all the ridiculous rules I have ever heard of this one took the cake.

The man that owned the lodge offered to let us use his old pickup truck to drive to the spring where he got water about two miles past the border, and told us to fill our jugs, then drive back to the road block and unload there, then bring the truck back. I wish I could remember his name, because he was really helpful that day and very generous.

We had to wait a week for the return pilot car to take us back to chicken. When we arrived the locals there had told us that there were always caribou on the Chicken Ridge trail. So we loaded up our wheelers and took off. Sixty miles later we arrived to what looked like the whole city of Fairbanks, all sitting on the tops of ridges on four and six wheelers of every make and description, and not a single caribou was in sight, not even an old track.

As always we went beyond the end of the trail, and wound up in a mining camp that was knee deep in muckity mud. The kind of mud which sucks the machine down, and won't let go. We winched, and winched, finally getting them free after many hours of hard work. We were covered from head to foot in mud, all you could see that was human, was our eyes. On the way out I had to overhaul Steve's starter in a hard rain, then my chain broke and I had to stop in the mud and put a new one on that I had with me. We were sick and tired of Chicken Ridge, we never saw one single caribou or moose track, let alone a live animal.

We loaded up and headed to our moose hunting country at mile forty two of the Tok cutoff. It was still raining hard and had been the whole trip. We loaded our camp on the wheelers and took off. The trail was as bad as it gets for 6-wheelers but we made it in to our regular camping spot.

We stayed there three days and it never quit raining. Now we are used to rain but these were torrential down pours, like the ones I have seen in Louisiana during a hurricane. We got tired of it, and not seeing any moose, we loaded up and headed back to the road. On the way out, the huge ten man tent I was so proud of, fell off the back of the wheeler and got wound up in the chain, and I had to cut it out. Steve's front axle housing had broken in half, and his chain kept coming off in the worst mud holes. It was a miserable trip out.

We drove back toToke Junction where Steve tried to buy another axle housing, but there was not one to be had in the state. We saw an ad for a small older motor home, and went to look at it as it had a four KW generator and was worth what the guy was asking for it. We were surprised that everything worked like new, so we bought it for six hundred dollars. Steve said, "Hell we can camp in it until the rain stops." A good idea except for the fact that it didn't stop raining.

When we finally got tired of the rain, we decided to go back home and give up.... beaten by Mother Nature. I do have to say that it was nice camping in that motor home though, with the heater and cook stove.

I talked it over with Liz after Steve went home and decided I needed to do an Indian cleansing, that I had done something to mess up my mojo. I call it that simply because I don't know what else to call it. We had driven more than a thousand miles without seeing a single game animal in country that was famous for having lots of animals. I know it sounds silly to most folks but I really believed that I had offended the animal kingdom somehow. I must have wasted some portion of animal meat or fish at some point since I had last hunted. On this trip I never felt that old connection I used to get when I was in the woods hunting. I never got that "Tuned In" feeling that was so familiar to me.

So I did the prayer and cleansing thing with smoke from a burning willow branch just like the Indians do. I prayed to my ancestors and the God of the universe to take this curse from me, and restore my hunting abilities, then I washed myself with the smoking branch. I got this strange feeling it was working, but I do have to admit that I felt more than a little silly when I started the ceremony.

I had bought a Browning compound bow the previous year and target practiced until I was deadly accurate. I could put all of the target arrows in the bull's eye at ten yard increments up to sixty yards. I had wanted to get a moose with it but of course I had to see one first.

The very next morning after the cleansing, I went out to start the generator in the shed, and I saw movement out of the corner of my eye. There were two moose standing about twenty feet away, but my bow was in the house. When I moved, the younger bull ran off. The other just stood there watching me while I ran in the house, and got my bow, changed the target point to a broadhead, and knocked an arrow. I ran back out and was pleasantly surprised that he was still standing there in the same spot. As I got within twenty feet of him, he started to walk parallel to me, then he broke into a slow motion trot, still not fifty feet away. I aimed and shot. The arrow hit him behind the heart shot and in his stomach, because I hadn't led him enough. Oh crap I thought, this is going to be a messy gutting job. He traveled another hundred feet, stopped, laid down, and died within ten minutes.

When Liz and I gutted it, the arrow had somehow went through the moose without hitting any of the gut sack. The cavity was clean as a whistle. I couldn't find anything that was pierced enough to have killed him, and I looked and looked. Heart, liver, kidneys and lungs were all intact. The arrow had entered way to low to have hit a spinal nerve.

To this day I can't understand or explain how it happened. When you looked at the point of entry.... then the other side where the arrow point was sticking out.... the gut sack was directly between the two points. The stomach was not pierced and, there was no artery cut, the cavity showed no blood, and there was not a blood trail or puddle of blood anywhere to be found. It is one of the biggest mysteries I have ever come across, and one that I still wonder about, because that big old broad head was sharp and should have sliced and diced all the way through the moose.

I did feel as though my mojo had been restored, and I

definitely want to keep it that way.

It is my belief that I should not kill any living thing which I do not intend to eat, whether it be fish, foul, or animal. Otherwise my mojo will suffer.

By the time I was in my late teens I had developed a somewhat similar way of thinking as the Native Americans, in that I never want to offend the spirit of any animal, and will do whatever it takes to keep that from happening… no matter how silly I appear to other men.

*

To any law enforcement that may read this book, please know that I am the biggest liar that ever lived.

13883380R00042

Made in the USA
Charleston, SC
06 August 2012